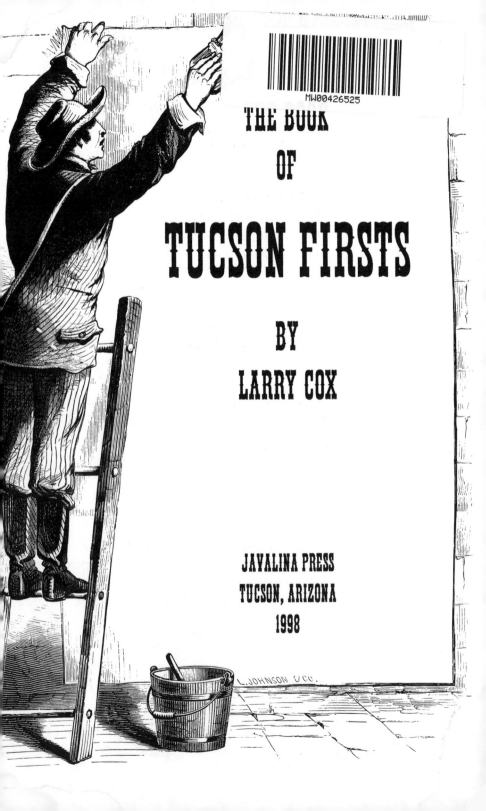

THE BOOK
OF
TUCSON FIRSTS

BY
LARRY COX

JAVALINA PRESS
TUCSON, ARIZONA
1998

MW00426525

THE BOOK OF TUCSON FIRSTS
By Larry Cox
Copyright 1998 by Javalina Press
P.O. Box 65436
Tucson, Arizona 85728

First edition 1998
Five thousand copies

Library of Congress Card Catalogue number
98-96671

ISBN 0-9667658-0-X

Soft cover $14.95

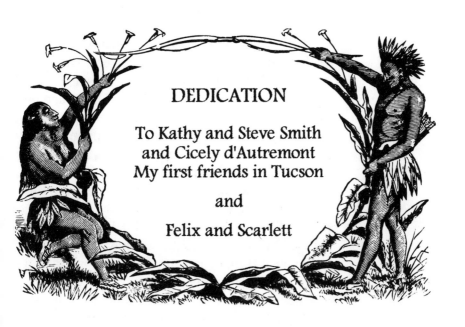

DEDICATION

To Kathy and Steve Smith
and Cicely d'Autremont
My first friends in Tucson

and

Felix and Scarlett

ACKNOWLEDGMENTS

This book would not have been possible without the help, encouragement and cooperation of many people.

My deepest appreciation is extended to Debra Shelton and her fine staff of researchers at the Arizona Historical Library in Tucson. Dana DaLong of the Tucson City Clerk's Office and both Tony Cox of the Tucson Police Department and Randy Ogden of the Tucson Fire Department were especially helpful. Much praise is due Kristin Brown who taught me that the computer is not necessarily the devil's tool. I had many questions about early television in Tucson and Jeff Sales of KOLD-TV and Mike Sears of KUAT-TV helped me find the answers. Ethel Bufkin, widow of the late Donald Bufkin, gave me kind permission to use his 1870 map of Tucson.

One of the most pleasant afternoons spent in researching my book was with Sister Alberta Cammack, CSJ, at St. Mary's Hospital. She gave me invaluable information about Tucson's first doctor and the struggle to build the town's first hospital.

I also received help from Barbara Beyer of Tucson Electric Power Company, the staff of the Tucson Public Library, Renee Downing of the Arizona Daily Star, and the research staffs of both the Tucson Citizen and the University of Arizona.

Jan Catt-Santiago was always there, as both proofreader and friend. Suzanne Myal's words of encouragement came just at the right time and were appreciated.

AN INTRODUCTION, AN EXPLANATION AND EVEN AN APOLOGY

I moved to southern Arizona from Colorado in 1996. I had lived in the High Country and the simple truth is I got a little weary of scraping ice and clearing snow even during the summer months. One July 4th, while flipping hamburgers in the snow, it suddenly occurred to me that not every place in the United States had that kind of cold weather. The search for a new home was soon underway.

Tucson wasn't on my initial list of places to consider. One evening, while watching the late-night news on television in a Tucson motel, I heard a local story that changed my mind about the Old Pueblo. A drunk had robbed an adult bookstore. The masked bandit had been armed with a cactus. Where else could that have happened? I knew, after hearing that story, Tucson was, indeed, my kind of town.

I have always been fascinated by history. I was raised in a region steeped in stories about the Civil War. Later, I lived in the small mining community of Colorado where the Rocky Mountain gold rush had begun. After my move to Arizona, I found myself spending more and more time at the Historical Society Library in Tucson. Through clippings, photographs and other reference materials, the early history of southern Arizona came alive for me.

Several sources I found while researching my book merit special mention. Bonnie Henry's newspaper columns as published in the Arizona Daily Star are exceptional. She is able to capture the spirit of Tucson's past. "Tucson" published by Bernice Cosulich in 1953 is still one of the best

5

books written about the early history here. The fascinating work by C.L. Sonnichsen, "Tucson: The Life and Times of an American City," is both detailed and definitive. For flavorful accounts of the Hispanic experience in Tucson, I highly recommend both "Los Tucsonenses" by Thomas E. Sheridan and Patricia Martin's wonderfully written "Images and Conversations: Mexican Americans Recall a Southwestern Past." The best collection of information was, of course, the original materials contained in the archives of the Arizona Historical Society Library in Tucson. The staff patiently helped me ferret out most of the information used in this book. Debra Shelton and her excellent people went beyond the call of duty and rarely flinched when I often stepped to the counter looking for some obscure piece of almost impossible to find information. I can't praise the people of the Arizona Historical Society Library enough. The collection is a treasure trove for anyone interested in our colorful history.

Writing this book hasn't always been easy. There were sometimes three or four different versions of an event and it was often impossible for me to determine the truth with absolute certainty. A good example, was the problem I had tracking down the year the first motion picture was shown in Tucson. In three separate accounts the dates are given as 1903, 1905 and 1906. Which was correct? After several weeks of frustration, it finally came down to my best guess. The title of that first film was "The Great Train Robbery" which was released in 1903 and I assumed it would have been shown here that same year and so went with the earlier date. Is 1903 absolutely accurate without question? No, it was simply my best guess. Although I have tried to remain as close to the truth as possible, there are without a doubt errors in my book. The errors are mine and mine alone. For any inaccuracies, let me apologize in advance.

My book is meant to be a fun, informal history. If it creates enough interest with the reader that it prompts a visit to the excellent research collection or the fine museum of the Arizona Historical Society, my book will be, at least in my eyes, a successful effort. Most of all, I hope you enjoy "The Book of Tucson Firsts."

Several months ago, I finally tossed out my snow shovel and donated my parka to a charity. I'm here to stay. I love Tucson.

Larry Cox
Tucson, Arizona

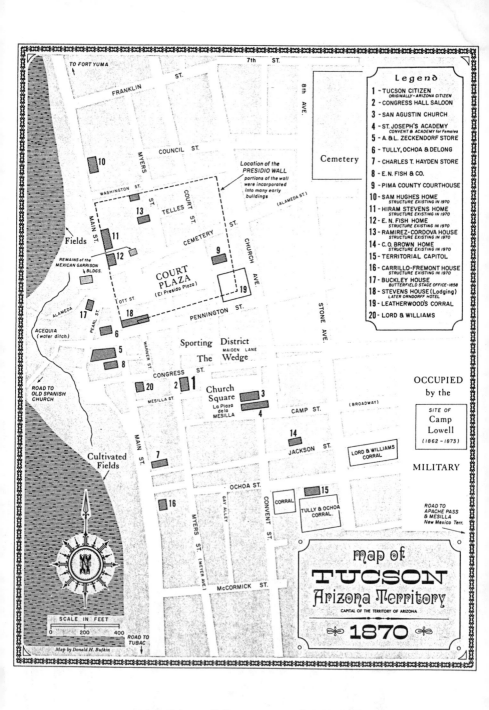

Donald Bufkin's Map of 1870 Tucson.
Used through the courtesy of Ethel M. Bufkin.

ADULTERY

The year was 1802. Jose Siqueiros was assigned to the Presidio in Tucson as an armorer. His wife -- Maria Jesus Arguelles -- was caught in an act of adultery with another soldier. Soon everyone knew and Jose was furious. So furious, he drafted a letter charging his wife with adultery. He submitted his letter to the Presidio chaplain.

After filing his complaint, Jose had second thoughts. The Presidio could be a lonely place without the comfort of a woman, even if that woman happened to be just a tad bit unfaithful. He met with the chaplain who advised Jose to "dimittite et dimitretur vobis" or forgive as you would be forgiven. He did. Maria cleaned up her act and they settled down together again as husband and wife. No further complaints ever surfaced concerning the marital problems of Jose and Maria but it was, in fact, the earliest case of recorded adultery in Tucson.

AIR CONDITIONING

It's hard to imagine a Tucson summer without air conditioning but there was a time -- and not so long ago -- when refrigerated air simply did not exist in the Old Pueblo.

Air conditioning finally arrived in 1933. A team of six engineers from Los Angeles began an installation on the roof of the Fox Theatre. The huge unit was a $60,000 investment, an incredible amount of money during the early 1930s. The air conditioning unit continued to function for over 40 years. In

9

fact, the original system was still working when the Fox finally closed its doors in 1974.

AIRPLANE FLIGHT

It was a marvel and it was also a financial bust. Emanuel Drachman was quite a promoter and he had an idea which he thought couldn't lose.

Drachman and members of the Chamber of Commerce announced plans for the Tucson Air Show of 1910. They were so confident, a guarantee of $2,000 plus half the gate were offered to Charles "The Bird Man" Hamilton to fly his airplane as the highlight of the show. There had been other earlier attempts to fly in Tucson. One craft, pulled by a horse, was launched one afternoon for a few minutes during the autumn of 1909. Hamilton's turn in the sky would be one of the earliest public exhibitions of flight in the region.

Charles "The Bird Man" Hamilton at Elysian Grove in 1910.

The two-day air show began January 19, 1910. A group of people gathered at an old baseball field at Elysian Grove, a site occupied today by the Carrillo Intermediate School. Hamilton made a few adjustments to his craft and then, after signaling his assistant, he coasted several hundred feet through the dust and finally slowly lifted into the air. He continued his flight for almost four miles and achieved a speed of just over 35 miles per hour.

Although an admission was charged, most of the spectators watched from outside the fenced compound. This created a much smaller gate than had been anticipated. The 1910 air show was not a financial success.

AIR RAID SIRENS

The cold war was taken very seriously in Tucson.

As children were taught to "duck and cover" during drills in school, some adults were concerned enough, they actually constructed bomb shelters in their homes.

In 1952, Louis Menager was appointed to organize the Tucson Civil Defense Office. His first order of business was to install air raid sirens throughout the downtown area. Within five years, the testing of sirens had become commonplace. Eleven sirens were on-line by 1957 with four additional ones in reserve. The peak of preparedness was in 1959 when 20 sirens were operational.

ALCOHOLICS ANONYMOUS

In 1943, America was occupied with World War II. Ham was a 35 year-old military officer who was stationed at Davis-Monthan Air Force Base and in addition to the war, he was also in conflict with himself. He was an alcoholic.

Ham was determined to do something about his problem. He met Frank, a tailor at Varsity

Cleaners. On the evening of February 22, 1943, the two men vowed to help each other. Although the national chapter of Alcoholics Anonymous had been formed in New York in 1935, the first Tucson chapter began with Ham and Frank that February night in 1943.

AMERICAN FLAG

Although it was made of rags and wasn't exactly accurate, it was -- at least in the hearts of the people in Tucson -- a genuine American flag.

It was sewn from scraps and hoisted near the present day Court Plaza the morning of December 16, 1846. A battalion of Mormons raised the flag and then marched away two days later.

Following the Gadsden Purchase nine years later, a group cheered as a second American flag fluttered from a large mesquite pole as the last of the Mexican garrison evacuated the Presidio in February of 1855.

AMBULANCE SERVICE

Delbert Aegerter moved to Tucson in 1946. With his brother, William, they pooled their money and purchased two used Cadillac vehicles. The city's first private ambulance service was in business.

A&A Ambulance Service continued until it was eventually purchased by Rural-Metro Fire Department. Delbert Aegerter died in 1990 and is buried in Evergreen Cemetery on North Oracle Road.

AMUSEMENT PARK

It wasn't exactly Disneyland but it did keep the citizens of early Tucson entertained.

Alexander Levin lived in a small adobe house on Mission Street near Pennington. He built a brewery near a well at the rear of his house. He saw great potential and soon added a beer garden with an adjoining saloon and billiard hall.

By the 1870s, Levin's Park had expanded to include a bullring, bowling alley, open dance pavilion, a restaurant and even a small theatre. There was an arbor with a flower garden that was a little slice of heaven for young lovers. The public park was one of the most popular places in town, especially during the hot summer evenings of the 1870s and 80s.

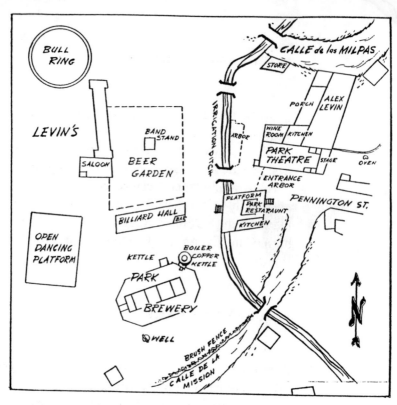

Levin's Park during the 1870s.

ARMORY

Although there were militia drills in a crude adobe structure at Levin's Park as early as the 1880s, the first structure built expressly for that purpose wasn't dedicated until 1914.

The Armory, which was constructed on South Sixth Avenue, was the home of both E and H Companies of the Arizona National Guard. The building included a large hall with a shooting range in the basement. The Armory was demolished in 1975.

AUTOMOBILE

Dr. Hiram W. Fenner saw his first automobile at a circus in Tucson in about 1899. He was so fascinated, he immediately ordered one of the new fangled horseless carriages for himself.

Since there were no automobile dealers in Arizona, Dr. Fenner had to order his Locomotive Steamer from the plant back east. The contraption was shipped to Tucson by rail.

The morning it arrived at the depot, a large crowd gathered to gawk. It was carefully unloaded and everyone pushed forward to get a better look.

Dr. Fenner and his locomotive steamer.

Dr. Fenner tinkered with the automobile for almost 30 minutes before he finally got it fired up and started. The crowd cheered as he climbed behind the crude steering stick and drove away in a cloud of dust. Dr. Fenner's triumph came to an abrupt halt when he ran smack into a sahuaro several blocks from the station. Except for the loss of a little pride, no other damage was done.

In 1905, Dr. Fenner was issued Tucson's first driver's license.

AUTOMOBILE RACE

On New Year's Day in 1911, a flag dropped and over a dozen automobiles zoomed away from a starting point on Speedway Blvd.

The drivers -- or scorchers as they were called -- raced along a route which went from Euclid and Speedway to Wilmot, Wilmot to Broadway, Broadway to Euclid and then back to the finish line on Speedway. The three top drivers, who reached speeds estimated to be more than 40 miles per hour, received prizes totaling $100. It was Tucson's first organized automobile race.

BABY CARRIAGE

Charles O. Brown was barely twelve years old when he left his home in Illinois to head west. After a brief time in Texas, Brown explored the gold fields of California. He settled in Tucson in about 1858.

He married Clara Borrean in 1864 while visiting Mesilla, New Mexico. Both Clara and Charles returned to Tucson to begin their family.

Shortly after his first child was born, Brown ordered a baby carriage, the first ever seen in Tucson. It was shipped by wagon and was the envy of every mother in town.

Charles Brown and his family moved into a house at 40 West Broadway in 1868. Brown also opened the Congress Hall Saloon on the corner of Meyer and Congress Streets that same year.

A million miles
of *sunshine* in
TUCSON
("Too-sŏhn")

BANK

Imagine trying to operate a retail business without a bank.

Lionel Jacobs, and his brother Barron, opened a mercantile store in Tucson in 1867. The lack of a bank created a serious hardship for the two businessmen. Although, Jacobs & Company was a retail store, the brothers began offering banking services as early as 1870.

In 1875, they issued certificates of deposit and maintained several dozen savings accounts for their most valued customers. As the banking services began to expand, both Lionel and Barron Jacobs set about to establish a full-service bank.

The Pima County Bank opened January 2, 1879, on the corner of Meyer and Congress Streets. It was a great location. It was just across the street from the Congress Hall Saloon, one of the most popular gathering places in town.

With the opening of the new bank, people in Tucson could secure credit. Short-term loans, usually of a 30-day duration, were available at two to three percent interest assessed per month.

During the next three decades, the bank changed names several times. In 1882, it was chartered as the First National Bank of Tucson. Three years later, it became the Bank of Tucson and in 1890 closed and re-opened as Arizona National Bank.

BASEBALL

One of the earliest baseball games in Tucson was played the afternoon of February 22, 1898. Athletes from the University of Arizona challenged a team of businessmen from downtown. After several hours of hard play, the town team was the winner with a final score of 25-23.

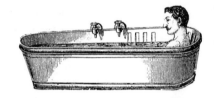

BATHTUB

Charles O. Brown was the successful owner of the Congress Hall Saloon. He served on the first city council, liked to wear snappy clothes and even enjoyed a bath now and then. Even though most people in Tucson during the 1870s were content to jump in the nearest irrigation ditch when they felt the urge to bathe, this quaint practice would not do for the fastidious Mr. Brown.

He saw just what he wanted in a catalogue: a zinc bathtub. He ordered it and a number of weeks later it arrived and was taken to the Brown family home at 40 West Broadway. Although the zinc tub had to be hand-filled with buckets of water, Brown and his expanding family were pleased with the new purchase.

Some of the wags in town shook their heads. A bathtub. What was Tucson coming to?

The Albert Steinfeld Mansion.

BATHTUB (MODERN PLUMBING)

The first bathtub connected to running water was installed in the mansion of department store tycoon, Albert Steinfeld. The tub was in use as early as the spring of 1904. Albert's wife, Bettina, was the talk of her friends after they saw her new porcelain tub with bright brass fixtures. The Steinfeld mansion is at 300 North Main Street near Franklin.

BICYCLE RACE

The first bicycle race from Tucson to Phoenix was a test of strength, both for the riders as well as the equipment.

Twenty-seven riders began the race in Tucson one May morning in 1921. The route covered over 140 miles of rutty dirt roads, which snaked through the desert. Punctured tires and breakdowns were commonplace. Of the 27 racers who entered the race, only three managed to make it to the finish line in Phoenix.

19

Hube Yakes, who rode a bicycle equipped with balloon tires, finished the race in eight hours and 51 minutes. He claimed the first prize of $500. James Rorex and Emile Lyall also completed the race. Both had ridden bicycles with narrow tires. Because of the heat and road hazards, the racers were monitored closely by officials who followed in automobiles. The cars were loaded with ample water and even spare tires.

A boy and his bicycle in the 1890s.

BICYCLE WRECK

As more and more bicyclists took to the streets of Tucson during the 1890s, public safety became a major concern. Although stern warning were issued, most went unheeded. It took an accident to bring about change.

One June morning in 1894, two bicycle riders collided just outside Old Main on the University of Arizona campus. Both riders were injured, one seriously. Witnesses claimed that both riders did not obey simple traffic rules.

A month later, the Tucson City Council passed mandatory speed limits for bicycle riders. Just days after the new law went into effect, a bike rider was arrested and brought before a city judge. The culprit was charged with "riding the tandem at too great a speed and so knocking down a little child." After a severe tongue lashing by the judge, the rider was fined one dollar and released.

BIRTH - ANGLO

Harry Arizona Drachman was born February 3, 1869, at the family home on West Alameda Street, just across the street from the present day city hall. He was the son of Mr. and Mrs. Phil Drachman and was the earliest recorded Anglo birth in Tucson. Harry Arizona Drachman lived in Tucson until his death in 1951.

BLACK ATHLETE - UNIVERSITY OF ARIZONA

Fred Batiste was the first black athlete to letter in sports at the University of Arizona. In 1948, he earned a football letter and, two years later, received one for his achievements in track.

BLACK CLUB

In 1884, the first black social club was established in Tucson. The Wide-a-Wake Colored Club was both social and political in nature.

BLACK COWBOY

Harvey Merchant was born in Texas and even at an early age he wanted to be a cowboy.

He arrived in Tucson in about 1870. He found a job as a dishwasher at a cattle ranch in southern Arizona but he didn't remain a cook's assistant for long. By 1875, he had earned the reputation of being one of the best bronc busters in all of Pima County.

BLACK DENTIST

Dr. Floyd Thompson opened a dental clinic on South Main Avenue in 1946. He spoke fluent Spanish and not only saw patients in Tucson, he also helped migrant workers throughout southern Arizona.

Dr. Thompson was born in Houston, Texas, but was raised in Tucson where he attended Dunbar and Tucson High School. He graduated from Howard University in 1942. During WWII, he served as a first lieutenant in the Army Dental Corps.

Dr. Thompson was active in efforts of desegregate what is now the Tucson Unified School District. He was a lifelong member of the National Association for the Advancement of Colored People (NAACP). He died in 1992 following a short illness. He was 78 at the time of his death.

BLACK ENTERTAINER

Charley Williams loved to play the banjo.

Throughout the 1870s, he played at public functions and often

22

Banjo Dick.

presented concerts at Levin's Park. He was one of the first, if not the first, black entertainers in Tucson.

"Banjo Dick," as he was known professionally, was a confirmed bachelor throughout his life. He lived alone, saved his money and opened a small shoeshine parlor in Nogales in 1891.

BLACK HOMESTEADER

Joe Mitchell arrived in Tucson in 1870. He homesteaded 160 acres just south of town. Although he was a barber by trade, he supplemented his income by raising chickens and selling eggs.

BLACK PHYSICIAN

Dr. Alden B. Thompson was raised in Texas. He attended Howard University and interned at Freeman's Hospital, both in Washington, DC. He took his post graduate training in surgery at Stanford with advanced studies as the University of Colorado School of Medicine, the Mayo Clinic and Philadelphia General Hospital. As far as can be determined, he was not related to Dr. Floyd Thompson, the town's first black dentist, who was also from Texas.

Dr. Thompson set up his medical practice in Tucson in 1928. He continued until illness forced his retirement in 1964. He died that same year at the age of 64.

BLACK RECREATION CENTER

The first black recreation center in Tucson was at Estevan Park. The facility opened in 1943 and was named for the Moroccan guide who explored what is now the American southwest in 1536.

BLACK SETTLERS

Wiley and Hannah Box arrived in Tucson in about 1855. Work was scarce and they accepted what few odd jobs were available. Wiley Box tried his hand as a freighter and his wife gathered mineral specimens that she sold as curios.

Through hard work and determination, they saved enough money to buy a home on Convent Street.

Wiley Box died following a practical joke that went awry. One evening while Box napped in front of his home, a friend tied a rag soaked in kerosene to his big toe and then set it on fire. He only meant to startle his friend but his prank led to blood poisoning terminating with Boxes' death several weeks later.

BLACK VISITOR

The first man, not native to the area, to see southern Arizona -- and perhaps the site which is present day Tucson -- was Estevan, a Moorish guide traveling with Fray Marcos de Niza, a Spanish explorer. They visited the American southwest in 1536. Since Estevan traveled several miles ahead of the exploration party, he was the first to actually step across the boundary that is now the southern Arizona-New Mexico border. Since he also passed between the Pima villages and Florence, he must have been the first non-native American to see that area, too.

Did Estevan make it to Tucson? No one knows for certain but even if he didn't, he did explore throughout southern Arizona and must have gotten tantalizing close. After over 450 years he gets the benefit of the doubt.

BOOK

The first book published in Tucson was not destined to be a bestseller.

Thirty-one delegates attending a provisional constitutional convention for the proposed territory met in Tucson in 1860. The meeting led to the publication of the first book printed in Arizona. It was "Constitution and Schedule of the Provisional Government of the Territory of Arizona, and the Proceedings of the Convention Held at Tucson." The book was the work of J. Howard Wells.

BOWLING ALLEY

A ten-pin bowling alley opened in about 1871 at Leopoldo Carrillo's Elysian Grove Park on South Main near 17th Street.

BRASS BAND

Almost every little town in American during the 1880s had a band shell and a brass band. Brass bands and patriotic marches were the rage. It was the era of John Philip Sousa.

Tucson quickly fell into step in 1880 when Anton V. Grossetta formed his band. Fred Ronstadt joined, too, and was a major asset. Not only could Ronstadt play several instruments, he could also arrange music.

BUSINESS DISTRICT

In 1858, Tucson's business district consisted of three mercantile stores, two butcher shops and two blacksmiths. Although no saloons existed as such, tequila by the drink or by the quart could be purchased in the mercantile establishments.

Business ads from 1881.

CAPITOL

The first seat of government for the Territory of Arizona in Tucson was in a series of crude adobe buildings on Ochoa Street just off Stone Avenue. The structure had a mud roof with a packed earth floor. The rented space had several small rooms with two larger ones for members of both the upper and lower houses of government.

The structure was so cramped, most legislators met informally at the Congress Hall Saloon. Many have suggested that Arizona's best laws were those which were hatched in the smoke-filled ambiance of Charles Brown's saloon.

The Arizona Territorial Capitol in Tucson, 1867-1877.

CATHOLIC CHURCH

Although worship services were conducted much earlier, the first Catholic Church wasn't built in Tucson until 1863.

Father Fray Donato Rogieri was a Franciscan from New Mexico who started the project but he did not live long enough to see its completion. Father Rogieri was killed during an Apache Indian attack in 1866.

Despite his death, work continued until the walls were finally completed in 1868. A convent was added just south of the main structure. Seven nuns of St. Joseph Carondelet opened St. Joseph's Academy for girls there in 1870. San Agustin Church was demolished in 1936. Parts of the original façade were utilized in the front entrance of the Arizona Historical Society Museum at 949 East 2nd Street.

Father Peter Bourgade, who became the first Catholic bishop in Tucson, was instrumental in the purchase of land on Stone Avenue between Ochoa and Corral Streets. A cathedral was started at the site in 1890 and dedicated seven years later. St. Augustine's Cathedral is located at 192 South Stone Avenue.

CATHOLIC MISSION

San Xavier del Bac was the earliest mission in Tucson, founded in 1692. A primitive structure was built in about 1700 and replaced some 90 years later.

San Cosme del Tucson was founded by Father Eusebio Francisco Kino in 1699. San Agustin del Tucson was constructed in 1757 but was replaced by a second structure in 1776. A second Presidio church was in use in Tucson after about 1800.

CEMETERY

Where was the first cemetery in Tucson? Since the area has been occupied for hundreds of years, it is impossible to answer with absolute accuracy.

Evergreen Cemetery.

The Presidio was established in 1776, bordered roughly by the present streets of Pennington, Washington, Church and North Main. The Presidio cemetery was located not far from the intersection of Alameda and Church Streets. In 1929, and again in 1970, construction workers discovered human remains in the area that dated back to the days of the Presidio.

The first municipal cemetery was located on East Alameda, then known as Cemetery Street. The cemetery was within an area bordered by 7th Street, North Stone Avenue and North Sixth. Records are sketchy but burials were conducted there as early as 1860. The cemetery closed in 1875.

After the closure of the Alameda site, a new cemetery was developed on Court Street between North Main Street and North Stone Avenue, then known as North 8th Avenue, Speedway and Second Street. The Court Street Cemetery closed in 1907.

Evergreen Cemetery opened on North Oracle Road in 1907 and many of the graves from the Court Street Cemetery were moved to the new location. Evergreen Cemetery is still in use.

CENSORSHIP

Few attempts have been made to censor books and publications in Tucson. One of the most interesting incidents, however, occurred in 1938. The controversy centered around an issue of Life Magazine.

In April of 1938, Life Magazine published an illustrated article about pre-natal care. One of the photographs represented the birth of a child. Police Chief Chistopher Wollard took one look at the magazine and blew a gasket. He decided the issue was unfit and ordered it removed from the news stands of Tucson. His order created a demand. In fact, one news dealer reported that all 320 copies he had were snapped up the first day.

W.R. Mathews, the publisher of the Arizona Daily Star, saw nothing wrong with the issue and was appalled at the ban. Not only did he challenge the ban, he sold copies of the magazine in the lobby of the Star building. Mathews said he was against the ban because "city officials don't know where to draw the line" between obscenity and educational materials. The flap caused the April 1938, issue of Life to become one of the most popular magazines ever sold in the city of Tucson.

CENSUS

One of the first nose counts in Tucson occurred in 1821. Of the 395 people counted that year, most were military personnel and assigned to the Presidio.

The next count, conducted ten years later, recorded 465 people, a slight increase.

The census of 1856 was more precise. It showed that 400 Mexicans and 50 "others" lived in the immediate area.

In 1864, U.S. Marshal Milton B. Duffield counted 1,568 people in Tucson.

CHAMBER OF COMMERCE

As more and more tourists discovered the warm winter sunshine of Tucson, Levi Manning pushed to form a chamber of commerce.

Tourists sunbathing poolside in Tucson in the 1940s.

In 1896, Manning, and a group of businessmen who shared his enthusiasm, met for the first time to organize a chamber. Manning was a businessman who was invested in mining and cattle. He was elected the first president of the Tucson Chamber of Commerce. Several brochures were immediately published which promoted both the mild climate and the healthy business community of the area.

Manning was elected mayor of Tucson in 1915. He ran on an anti-gambling, anti-vice ticket. He died in California in 1935.

Healthy recreation
in sunny TUCSON!

CHAIN GANG

Charlie Meyer was a pioneer druggist who thought he had just the right prescription to combat crime in early Tucson -- chain gangs.

During the 1870s, when Meyer was appointed justice of the peace, he had his work cut out for him. A traveler described Tucson in 1864 as "literally a paradise for devils." Meyer was concerned not only about crime but the filthy streets as well. He decided to take on both problems with a novel plan.

When someone was found guilty in Meyer's court, the culprit was often sentenced to a certain time on Charlie's chain gang. Crime decreased and the streets of Tucson showed a dramatic improvement.

Charlie Meyer.

Although Meyer did not have formal training in law, he never let his lack of education get in his way when he was dispensing his unique brand of western justice. His rulings in court were not appreciated by everyone, however. A man approached Meyer's bench one afternoon and asked how much the fine was for hitting a man. Meyer replied twenty dollars. The man took out a twenty-dollar gold piece, placed it in front of the judge, then punched him in the nose.

Meyer had a reputation for being fair and he thought laws applied to everyone. One afternoon he even fined himself for speeding in his buggy.

CHINESE

By the 1860s, several Chinese businesses had opened in Tucson. Three brothers named Wong operated the O.K. Restaurant on Church Street near Mesilla. This was one of the earliest businesses owned and operated by Chinese in the Old Pueblo.

THE CONDUCTOR.

Business ads from the 1880s including two owned by Chinese.

35

Chinese farmers also leased land along the Santa Cruz River and soon were operating small produce farms.

A Chinese mission school opened on Ott Street and provided bilingual education for about two dozen students during the 1880s.

Chee Kung Tong, a secret Chinese fraternal society, also flourished during the 1890s here.

COCKFIGHTS

Cockfights were considered major sporting events in Tucson during the 1870s and 1880s. Sometimes special bleachers were constructed for spectators and heavy betting was commonplace.

One of the most publicized contests occurred just before Christmas in 1894. Maximo Zuniga pitted his cock against one owned by Pedro Vadillo. Over $150 was wagered on the fight which attracted over 50 people.

COFFEE

It took Tucson cooks a little time, and trial and error, before they managed to brew a good cup of coffee.

Granville and William Oury arrived in Tucson from Missouri in about 1856. William was a soldier, farmer and business manager for the Butterfield Stage Company. His brother was an attorney. Coffee was unknown in the Old Pueblo

36

when the Oury brothers brought some green beans to a local woman. "Cook us up some coffee," Granville said to the woman. She did just that. When the beans were boiled and failed to soften, she then tried frying them. When Oury returned later to see if his coffee was ready, the woman said, "Well, it's been cooking a long time but it seems awful tough yet." Coffee, along with tequila, soon became one of the favorite drinks of choice by the 1870s.

COUNTRY CLUB

Golf in Tucson during the 1930s.

Levi Manning, Frank Hereford and W.H. Barnes were three businessmen who were also close friends. They often lunched together. One afternoon in 1903, after polishing off a meal at a downtown hotel, Manning lamented to his friends that it was a shame Tucson didn't have a country club. His two friends agreed and within weeks plans were underway to open a club.

In January of 1904, the necessary paperwork was completed but the task was more difficult than the men had imagined. It took ten years before investors could be found, land secured and a crude golf course plotted.

During the Easter weekend of 1914, over 100 golfers tested the first nine holes of the "skin course." The rough desert terrain was a challenge to even the best golfers but it was a beginning.

Several months later, a clubhouse opened and nine additional holes of golf were added to the original course.

COURTHOUSE

County business was originally conducted in a small adobe building near the corner of Ott and Court Street. The small structure was replaced in 1881 with an ornate Victorian building near Court and Pennington.

In 1927, during a routine inspection, large structural cracks were discovered. A further search revealed that the old building was in danger of collapse. The time had come to finance and build a "modern" courthouse.

The Pima County Courthouse
shortly after it was built.

Roy Place designed the new courthouse, which he described as a mixture of Spanish colonial and Moorish designs. It was such a departure from the norm in Tucson, it was not without controversy. The new courthouse opened in 1929 and was built on the sites of the original county jail (1881) and Tucson Pioneer Hose Company #1 (1883)

CURVE BALL

Manny Drachman loved baseball.

He was fascinated by the techniques of the game. During the 1880s, a railroad telegrapher taught Manny how to throw a curve ball. Manny's curve ball was so fast, it soon became legend even outside of Arizona.

Manny Drachman's pitching skills eventually came to the attention of Charles Cominsky who offered Drachman a job with his St. Louis team. Drachman did love baseball but he enjoyed living in Tucson near his friends and family even more and declined the opportunity.

DANCE HALL

People in Tucson have always loved dancing. It probably began with Indians who danced around camp fires here hundreds of years ago. Mexican soldiers were taken by the quadrille and Victorians enjoyed a good polka or two under the stars at Levin's Park. With all this in mind, it's really no surprise that one of the earliest structures in town was a dance hall.

In 1862, Leopoldo Carrillo scouted the area and finally purchased a small piece of

Carrillo Gardens in 1887.

property near Mission Road. He set about clearing it that same year. A grove of cottonwood trees provided shade near several small springs that bubbled to the surface nearby. He called his park Elysian Grove.

Just inside the main entrance, he built a large saloon and beyond that, a dance hall. On warm summer nights, officers from Fort Lowell often whirled senoritas there to the Virginia reel or, perhaps, the latest waltz. After dancing, couples sometimes strolled through Carrillo's gardens to watch the reflections of the moon on a small lake not far from the hall.

It was a magical place. Each year, from August 28th through September 16th, Tucson celebrated Fiesta de San Agustin at the park. In addition to dancing, there was gambling, sporting events, puppet shows, concerts, an occasional political speech or two and, best of all, food.

DANCE HALL - BIG BAND ERA

Throughout the 1930s, the height of sophistication was to snuggle with a special sweetie on the polished dance floor of the Santa Rita Ballroom.

The glittering art deco décor was the perfect setting for some of the most famous dance bands in the country. The ballroom, which opened in 1905, was considered the first, truly elegant hall in the city The grand old hotel was the favorite Tucson watering hole for such celebrities as Clark Gable, Jimmy Stewart and John Wayne. Gregory Peck even rode his horse into the lobby of the Santa Rita Hotel one evening after a hard day's shooting in southern Arizona for the production of "Duel in the Sun."

41

***The Santa Rita
Ballroom***

The Blue Moon, across town on North Oracle Road, wasn't as posh as the Santa Rita but did feature outstanding regional bands and was often packed to the rafters during weekends. The hall had tin walls and hinged windows that swung out to allow air circulation. The floor was the main draw. The maple dance floor was considered one of the best in town.

During the 1930s, "taxi dancers" were featured at the Blue Moon. For ten cents a dance, a partner could be rented for a turn or two. Just to make certain everything was on the up and up, monitors maintained a careful watch.

The Blue Moon was destroyed by fire in 1947.

DENTIST

L. S. Barnes began his dental practice in Tucson in about 1874. He was probably the first to establish a dental practice in Tucson.

As painful as it may sound, there were no educational requirements to practice dentistry in Arizona Territory during the 1870s and 1880s. If you wanted to be a dentist, you simply announced that you were a dentist and began your practice.

The legislature of 1893 decided to put some teeth into the lax policies of the past. A law was passed that spring making it mandatory that all dentists had to meet certain criteria before a state license would be issued. Only one dentist in Tucson was able to meet the new standards.

Stone Avenue looking north from Congress Street in 1948.

DEPARTMENT STORE

Tucson's first stores were crude, small adobe huts with inventories limited to the bare essentials.

William, Aaron and Louis Zeckendorf were successful

43

merchants who operated a thriving mercantile store in Santa Fe. Following Aaron's death in 1862, the two surviving brothers decided to expand their operations to Tucson.

In 1869, the arrived in town with several wagons of goodies. Prices were high. For example, a can of beans sold for about a dollar, an incredible price considering the fact that most men didn't earn a dollar a day during the 1860s. Despite the stiff prices, the inventory quickly sold and the Zeckendorf brothers proved to themselves that there was a marketplace in southern Arizona.

William and Louis Zeckendorf were eventually joined in the business by their nephew, Albert Steinfeld. Steinfeld became a junior partner and by 1906 was the sole owner. Steinfeld's Department Store on Stone Avenue and Pennington Street was a landmark and helped define retail excellence in Tucson well into the 20th century.

DIME STORE

Tucson's first dime store was Kress. The store opened in 1911 on East Congress and was successful enough, it was soon joined by two others, Woolworth and McLellans.

Looking east on Congress Street in about 1950.

DIVORCE

One of the first orders of business for the First Territorial Legislature that met in Prescott in 1864, was to grant three divorces. Since the Catholic Church frowned on divorces, recourse had to be found through the state government. One of the divorces approved was for John Capron, a Tucson merchant.

DRAG STRIP

During the early years of this century, as more and more automobiles took to the streets of Tucson, it was only natural that drivers began testing the speed of their vehicles.

Young men -- called "scorchers" by their elders -- met ever so often to race along a stretch of flat road just east of the business district. The races became so frequent, the events were instrumental in the naming of the road -- Speedway.

DRIVE-IN THEATER

In 1939, construction began at an eleven-acre site on Sixth Avenue near 44th Street. Within a few short weeks, a sixty-foot movie screen was in place and engineers from RCA were busy testing the sound system.

Several hundred cars jammed the streets around the theater opening night, January 25, 1940. The main attraction was, of course, the theater. William Holden's screen performance in "Golden Boy" seemed almost incidental.

Admission at the Tucson Drive-In was thirty cents for adults, children under 12 ten cents. Even though it was successful, it became a casualty of World War II and closed during the 1940s.

DRUG STORE

Charlie Hermann Meyer was born in Germany in 1829. Although his medical training was limited, he arrived in Arizona in 1858, serving as an assistant surgeon to troops stationed in Tucson.

47

In 1861, he opened a drug store on West Congress Street.

He married Encarnacion Gonzales and together they had five children. Meyer died in 1903.

George Martin started a drug store chain. He was born in Ireland and immigrated to American when he was about 20 years old. He enlisted in the United States Army in 1851 and completed his

The George Martin Drug Store on Congress Street.

tour of duty in 1856.

He opened his first drug store in Yuma in 1872. He sold it in 1883 and opened a pharmacy in Tucson at 32 West Camp, now known as Broadway. The drug store eventually moved to 40 West Congress and was the first establishment in the Territory to have a soda fountain.

Martin soon expanded his operations to include a total of eight stores, seven of which were in Tucson.

DUDE RANCH

Tanque Verde Ranch wasn't exactly a dude ranch but it came close. During the 1860s, the ranch was located near the Rincon Mountains just outside of

The Double U Dude Ranch in 1940.

Tucson and was operated by the Carrillo family. It was a working cattle ranch. After being purchased by James P. Converse, the ranch occasionally allowed paying guests. It was a concept soon copied by other ranches in the area.

The Flying V Ranch was popular throughout the 1920s and was often featured in slick tourist brochures. It was 12 miles north of town in Rock Canyon. The Flying V offered tourists a taste of the old west including spicy beans and smoked beef. A guest cottage at the ranch during the 1940s often rented for about $55 per week.

Some dude ranches made extra money by hosting movie production companies. The 1941 feature film "Billy the Kid" with Robert Taylor was shot mostly on location at the Double U Ranch in the foothills of Tucson.

Other popular dude ranches in the Tucson area included the Arrow H, Picture Rock Ranch, Desert Willow, Rancho Rita Trails, Silver Bell Ranch, High Acres and the Diamond W.

A Ranch Vacation *This Summer?*

EARTHQUAKE

Just after two o'clock, the afternoon of May 3, 1887, the ground began to shake throughout southern Arizona. In Tucson, crockery crashed to the floor as many, filled with terror, fled into the streets. Although the earthquake and its tremors lasted only four minutes, it generated absolute fear in Tucson. The courthouse tower swayed and several buildings in town cracked but there was no loss of life.

The earthquake was centered some 30 to 50 miles south of Douglas. In Mexico, fifty-two people died in the quake, most of the casualties were in the small village of Bavispe, Sonora. The Richter Scale would not be introduced until 1900, but later estimates put the 1887 earthquake at about 7.2 at its center in Mexico.

Broken windows and damaged structures were reported in both Tombstone and Douglas following the event.

ELECTRIC LIGHTS

Candles and oil lamps were used for illumination in Tucson homes and businesses throughout the 1870s. Both were unsafe and neither provided much light.

In 1882, Tucson had a brief fling with gas lamps. Gaslights were an improvement but not much. The following year electric street lighting was tried but the company failed and its assets liquidated. The city once again returned to the use of gas.

50

Eventually, Tucson Electric Light and Power Company was formed and a plant constructed on North Church Street, across from the present day Pima County Courthouse. In 1886, the company was re-named Tucson Gas, Electric Light & Power.

Tucson had in use some 2,000 "incandescent lamps" by 1897. In addition to the lights, there were also 20 electric fans. By 1900, the electric company had 225 "subscribers" out of a total population of 13,000.

ELEVATOR

Tucson's most elegant hotel came about because of unwanted guests -- bedbugs.

After a tourist complained that bedbugs had infested most of the hotel rooms in the city, L.H. Manning set about to rectify the situation. He built a new hotel at Broadway and Scott that he named the Santa Rita after the mountain range near his ranch.

*The incredible
Santa Rita
Hotel.*

The Santa Rita Hotel was a marvel. In addition to having the first passenger elevator in the city, the 200-room hotel boasted a roof garden, telephones in each guest suite and that miracle of miracles -- modern plumbing.

The Santa Rita Hotel, which opened in 1904, slipped into decline and was demolished in 1972. It took three weeks to level the proud old structure. During its glory days, guests at the Santa Rita included such celebrities as Helen Hayes, Errol Flynn, Louis Armstrong, Paul Newman and John Wayne. David Janssen filmed scenes for his television series, "The Fugitive," in one of the bars in the hotel.

All that is left.

ENTERTAINERS - SPANISH

The earliest recorded Spanish entertainers in Tucson were members of small Mexican circuses which traveled throughout southern Arizona during the 1850s. The Salvine Circus, Cadena & Zepeda

Company and the Gallardo Acrobatic Troup were popular in Tucson throughout the 1870s. Other acts, which played southern Arizona, included ballerinas, gymnasts, tightrope walkers and clowns.

In 1875, the Campania Dramatica, under the direction of Jose Perez, presented the Spanish drama "Daughter and Mother, or Andres the Piper" to a capacity house at the Cosmopolitan Hotel of Tucson.

ESCALATOR

The first escalator was installed in the S.H. Kress' Five and Ten Cent Store on East Congress Street in 1955. It was an immediate hit, especially with children who saw the moving stairs as an amusement ride. The escalator was so popular with

youngsters, a monitor had to be hired during its first months of operation.

ELKS LODGE

It wasn't exactly a palace but it was home for the first Elks Lodge in Tucson. The Elks Lodge, BPOE No. 385, was organized in October of 1897. The first lodge was constructed in 1898 at 89 North Court Avenue. It was a sparse building with no electricity, no heating and no plumbing.

The first woman was inducted into Elks Lodge No. 385 was Lucille Polonis. She joined the lodge December 19, 1995.

EXECUTION

In 1880, Thomas Harper shot and killed John Talliday. Although Harper later claimed it had been an act of self-defense, he was found guilty by a Pima County jury and sentenced to death by hanging

The evening of July 7, 1881, Harper met briefly in his Tucson jail cell with Sheriff Robert Paul. He asked for a drink and a cigar.

The next morning, Harper had a light breakfast. He spoke for a few minutes with a priest and then requested to see the scaffold. He was so persistent a deputy finally took him into a hallway so he could see the execution site. He looked at it for about a minute and then returned to his cell. It was two o'clock and Harper had less than an hour to live.

About thirty minutes later, Harper was taken from his cell. Sheriff Paul and Tucson Chief of Police Adolph Buttner led the condemned man to the yard. Harper took a drink of water and then repeated once again that he had acted in self-defense.

A rope was quickly placed around his neck and a black hood pulled over his head. At eleven minutes before three o'clock, the afternoon of July 8, 1881, Harper was "launched into eternity" according to a Tucson newspaper account.

It was the first official execution in both Tucson and Pima County.

FARMERS

Just southwest of Miracle Mile near the Santa Cruz River, farmers grew crops over 1,200 years ago.

Piut dwellings, grain storehouses and communal ruins have been found proving that the Cienegas lived and farmed along the river at least as early as 700 B.C. Although the Cienegas, who are probably the early ancestors of the Hohokam, were skilled hunters, they relied heavily on agriculture growing various crops including maize.

Some archaeologists now actually believe that agriculture could have been practiced along the Santa Cruz River much earlier than had been originally assumed, perhaps as early as 1200 B.C.

FESTIVAL

The Fiesta de San Agustin was Tucson's first official celebration.

The fiesta usually began August 28th and included religious processions, fireworks, serious drinking, gambling, puppet shows, horse racing, sports events, an occasional bullfight, dancing, concerts and food.

The earliest celebrations were at Church Plaza on South Church Street at Camp (Broadway). As the festival grew in popularity, a larger area was needed. The fiesta was first moved to La Plaza de las Armes, then to Levin's Park and finally Carrillo Gardens. The Fiesta de San Agustin was discontinued in about 1900. The celebration ended, many said, because of an anti-gambling, anti-vice stance taken by city leaders. The new attitude simply drained the fun out of the festival and it expired.

FILM MAKERS

The Lubin Film Company on location in Southern Arizona.

A group of filmmakers arrived in Tucson from Chicago in 1910. They were lured to southern Arizona by the abundance of natural light and the mild winter climate.

They established the American Film Manufacturing Company and produced five movies, all westerns, during its first year. The San Xavier Mission was used as a backdrop in at least one of their films.

In 1911, the Lubin Film Company arrived. A small studio was constructed on North Stone Avenue and film production continued there until May of 1912.

Although the American Manufacturing Company was the first to make feature films in Tucson, the Lubin Film Company built the first movie studio with stage here.

FINGERPRINTS

Louis Ezekiels was a Tucson police officer who was fascinated by stories he read about crime detection through the use of fingerprints. He was convinced that fingerprinting could be a valuable tool, which might help officers throughout Arizona crack difficult cases.

In 1905, he also convinced his superiors and that same year the Tucson police Department set up its first fingerprinting lab.

FIRE DEPARTMENT

It took several spectacular fires during the 1870s to convince the newly incorporated city of Tucson to budget money for the organization of a fire department.

The Tucson Fire Department was officially formed in 1883. Chief Jack Boylen had a team of 45 volunteers. A two-story adobe structure on Church Street opened that summer and served as the

The Tucson Fireman in their spiffy new uniforms, circa 1900.

city's first firehouse. It was just north of the old courthouse.

Chief Boylen proudly displayed his total arsenal of fire fighting equipment that first day -- 22 rubber buckets, six axes, six pick axes and nine shovels.

Three years later, money was found to purchase a hand-drawn hook and ladder wagon.

In 1900, the first firemen were added to the city payroll. The Tucson Fire Department moved to 111-115 North Church Street in about 1901.

The Tucson Fire Department hose wagon in 1910.

FIREWORKS

The first fireworks were probably introduced in Tucson during the 1870s. By 1880, the shooting of fireworks had become commonplace during the Fiesta de San Agustin at Levin's Park

58

FOOTBALL GAME

The University of Arizona football squad challenged a team from town during the autumn of 1899. The two teams squared off the afternoon of November 20, 1899, at Carrillo Gardens. After two hours of tackling, passes and fumbles, the final score remained 0-0.

FOOTBALL - INTERCOLLEGIATE

The first intercollegiate football game in Arizona was played Thanksgiving Day in 1899. Tempe Normal School, now known as Arizona State University, trounced the University of Arizona squad with a final score of 11-2.

FUND DRIVE

Although people had probably passed the hat before for certain projects in Tucson, the first major campaign drive occurred in 1880 to benefit St. Mary's Hospital.

The drive raised money so that St. Mary's Hospital, the first such institution in the state, could be equipped and ready for its first day of service.

P.D. Quinn was a miner and he was one of the first people to donate. He dropped three dollars into the hat. A dance raised additional money several

weeks later. By April of 1880, $200 had been raised and the hospital opened and admitted its first patients May 1, 1880.

GASLIGHTS

The first gaslights in Tucson were installed near the old Courthouse in March of 1882. Clyde James was hired by the Tucson Gas Company to light the dozen or so lamps each evening. He wasn't married and lived in a small apartment at the gas works.

One of the first commercial customers to try the new fangled gaslights was the Arizona Daily Star. Several gaslights were installed in the editorial offices during the summer of 1882 so that the newspaper elves could toil into the night.

GAY BARS

Although before 1970, there were no gay bars in Tucson, there were several taverns that were "gay friendly."

The Downtowner Bar in the Roskruge Hotel was popular throughout the 1940s. Bill Cleveland was a popular bartender there and when he quit following a pay dispute and moved to the Congress Hotel in about 1948, his clientele moved with him.

The Patio Bar, then on Alameda near Church Street, was small and intimate. It featured a piano bar weekends and was popular with visitors from out-of-town.

The 1960s saw the opening of the Black Door Bar in the MacArthur Hotel, on Toole Street between Sixth and Congress.

GOLF COURSE - GRASS

Although a primitive "skin" golf course was being played at the Tucson Country Club as early as 1914, the first course with grass wasn't completed until about 15 years later.

The El Rio Country Club developed 120 acres northwest of town. A.C. Hooper was hired to plan the links. Grass was carefully planted and watered. The new "greens" opened November 1, 1929, just a week following the stock market crash. Corbett served as president of the new club and managed to flush out some 250 members despite the bleak economic times.

The Municipal Golf Course in 1930.

GROCERY STORE - CHAIN

Daisy and David Woon opened a small grocery store in Eloy during the 1940s. When they sold it, they re-located to Tucson. They used the proceeds from the Eloy sale to finance a grocery store in Tucson.

Farmer's Market was at 1333 North Miracle Mile. Hard work and long hours allowed the Woons to expand. Additional stores were opened at

Broadway and Sixth Avenue and East Irvington Road and South Sixth Avenue.

During the 1950s, the Woons sold their three stores to Rulon Goodman. The Goodman markets were the first grocery store chain in the city and were absorbed by ABCO.

HISTORICAL SOCIETY

In 1884, a group of old timers met in Tucson to form Arizona's first historical society. Even the organizational meeting was filled with controversy.

A majority wanted to exclude membership to anyone who had arrived in Arizona later than January 1, 1870. The measure was adopted following a howl of protest. Several of those present stomped out of the meeting in protest. The original stated purpose of the society was to "serve historical and humanitarian purposes."

HORSE RACE

Horseracing has always been an important part of Tucson's colorful past. Horseracing with serious betting became part of the local scene as early as the 1870s.

One of the earliest publicized races occurred September 2, 1877. Four horses were entered in the event which included a purse of $175. The winning horse was El Aladen Arabe ridden by Albert Steinfeld of department store fame. The other entries included El Ingrato, ridden by Ramon

Vasquel; El Ahuacate, ridden by Placido Ruelas; and El Relampago, ridden by Juan Bohorquez.

Juan Elias had a small store just outside the Presidio walls during the 1850s. He was a man who was especially proud of his horse flesh. In 1882, he challenged the Ruelas brothers to a race. During that April afternoon in 1882, over $3,000 was bet. Elias' horse finished dead last.

HOSPITAL

Bishop Salpointe had an almost impossible decision to make.

Just west of town, the good Bishop found himself nearing the completion of a building that he planned to use as a trade school for Indian youth in the area. Indians had even helped in the construction and most were looking forward to the new school and the opportunities it meant.

Then the railroad asked for a favor.

St. Mary's Hospital in 1920.

Bishop Salpointe was contacted to help establish a hospital for Tucson. After careful thought, Bishop Salpointe made his decision. Despite protests by some of the Indian workers, the new building was rededicated as a hospital.

In 1880, a fund drive, one of the first such drives ever in southern Arizona, raised almost $200. The money was used for supplies. A second campaign instigated by the Tucson Citizen raised even more money so that a windmill for water could be constructed on the site.

Through hard work and the determined grit of the Sisters of St. Joseph of Carondelet, St. Mary's Hospital opened its doors the first day of May in 1880. Eleven patients were admitted that day suffering from complaints which ranged from sore eyes to tomahawk injuries. The total budget for the hospital during its first month of service was $56.30.

HOSPITAL - CHARITY

Rev. Oliver E. Comstock was a Baptist minister who was touched by the homeless drifters he saw on the streets on Tucson during the years just before World War I. Many needed medical attention and few had the means to get adequate care.

In 1910, Rev. Comstock pooled his money and opened the "Comstock Mission." He provided food and shelter in addition to limited medical care. Within a year, he had acquired three tents, a pile of blankets and a small food bank. His charity work relied heavily on public donations. The Comstock Mission eventually became known as the Adams Street Mission.

HOSPITAL - VETERANS

*The Veterans'
Hospital of
Tucson just after
WWII*

Although there were earlier military hospitals at both the Presidio and at Fort Lowell, the first installation for veterans was in an abandoned park on North Oracle Road. During the 1920s, several old wooden buildings were retrofitted and a small number of veterans received medical help there. The facility was too small and could not meet the demand.

A new hospital was constructed on South Sixth Avenue and opened in 1928. The Veteran's Hospital in Tucson is one of the best such facilities in the country.

HOTEL

Visitors didn't always find accommodations in the Old Pueblo very inviting. During the 1850s, there were no hotels so anyone traveling through the area had to find sleeping space wherever. The wherever usually meant in the corral with the horses.

Although there weren't hotels, Tucson did have its priorities. There were numerous saloons. One cantina occupied the front portion of an adobe structure on Alameda Street. The bartender there sometimes rented cots in a back storage room for overnight guests. It wasn't exactly four star but it was Tucson's first tourist accommodations.

The Palace Hotel Saloon during the 1880s.

The Cosmopolitan Hotel was one of the first major hotels in town. It opened in 1869 and featured one of the town's first passive evaporative cooling systems -- wet rugs draped near open windows. The Palace Hotel opened a decade later with 55 guestrooms, a saloon and the absolute marvel of indoor plumbing. The Palace was also the first Tucson hotel to offer guests beds with both a mattress and box springs.

The city's most elegant hotel was constructed in 1904 because of unwanted visitors -- bedbugs.

When a tourist complained that hotel rooms throughout the city were infested with the little varmints, L.H. Manning built the lavish Santa Rita at Broadway and Scott Street. The wonderful old hotel was demolished in 1972.

HOUSE

The earliest private homes in Tucson were small, adobe huts which were built near the Presidio. They were crude and constructed in a style that later became known as the Sonoran tradition.

Later homes were constructed of exposed adobe brick, one story and built flush to the street. The homes had small windows, flat roofs and interior floors of packed earth. Most of the cooking was done in an exterior courtyard under a ramada.

City engineer Gustav Schneider drew a plan of the typical pre-1880 Tucson dwelling sometime during the 1930s. His drawing shows a roof of packed earth supported by layers of saguaro ribs and pine rafters. What is absent from the drawing is any indication of a closet. Most people only had two or three changes of clothing and they were usually kept in a cupboard or ropero.

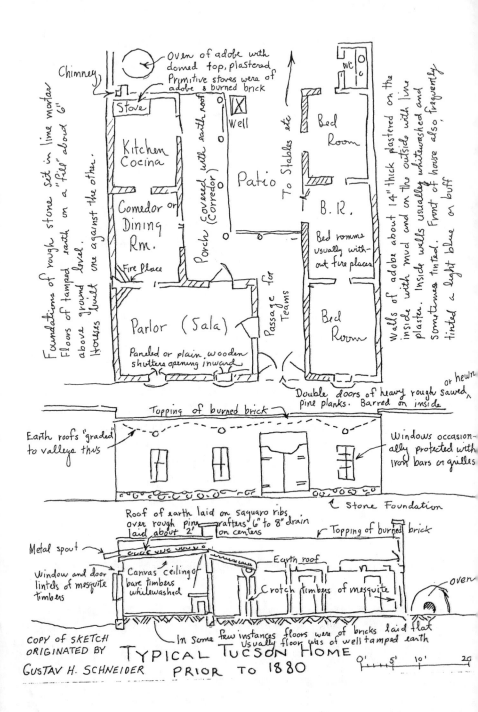

Chimney

Oven of adobe with domed top, plastered. Primitive stoves were of adobe & burned brick

Foundations of rough stone set in lime mortar. Floors of tamped earth on a "fill" about 6" above ground level. Houses built one against the other.

Stove

Kitchen Cocina

Comedor or Dining Rm.

Fire Place

Parlor (Sala)

Paneled or plain, wooden shutters opening inward

Porch (covered with earth roof) (Corredor)

Well

Patio

To Stables etc.

Passage for Teams

W.C.

Bed Room

B.R.

Bed rooms usually without fire places

Bed Room

Walls of adobe about 14" thick plastered on the inside with mud and on the outside with lime plaster. Inside walls usually whitewashed and sometimes tinted. Front of house also frequently tinted a light blue or buff

Double doors of heavy rough sawed, or hewn pine planks. Barred on inside

Topping of burned brick

Earth roofs "graded" to valleys thus

Windows occasionally protected with iron bars or grilles

Stone Foundation

Roof of earth laid on saguaro ribs over rough pine rafters 6" to 8" drain laid about 2' on centers

Metal spout

Topping of burned brick

Window and door lintels of mesquite timbers

Canvas ceiling of bare timbers whitewashed

Earth roof

Crotch timbers of mesquite

oven

COPY OF SKETCH ORIGINATED BY GUSTAV H. SCHNEIDER

In some few instances floors were of bricks laid flat. Usually floor was of well tamped earth

TYPICAL TUCSON HOME PRIOR TO 1880

0'   5'   10'   20'

68

The oldest house in Tucson still in existence is probably La Casa Cardova, 171-177 North Meyer Street, in the El Presidio neighborhood. Portions of the house were constructed as early as 1848.

ICE CREAM

An Italian from Sonora concocted the first ice cream ever tasted in Tucson in 1869.

A second batch was produced the following year.

The ice cream was made in a hand-cranked freezer and was served at Carrillo Gardens for a few short days in 1870. The supply was soon gone.

In 1875, an icehouse was built at Levin's Park that made ice cream more available for everyone. Well, maybe not everyone. Even with an adequate ice supply, ice cream still sold for about five dollars a quart at a time when most working stiffs were lucky if they earned a dollar a day.

The city's first ice plant opened during the 1880s and with the supply of manufactured ice, the dessert was finally within the reach of the average person.

JAIL

Tucson's first slammer of record was a small adobe room constructed near the southwest corner of the old Presidio. It was in use as a military prison before 1855. Large iron rings secured to the stone floor were used to lock down prisoners. For the unruly, a whipping post was just a few steps away.

In February of 1865, crime in Tucson was out of control and a more secure jail was needed. Hill d'Armitt, John Capran and Judge Trumbull Hayden raised money and ordered a specially built iron cage from a foundry in San Francisco. The cage consisted of three cells and was approximately twelve feet by seven feet. The cage arrived several months later and was quickly put into use. Tucson still had its share of ruffians but after the summer of 1865, many were caged ruffians.

JEWISH SYNAGOGUE

Temple Emmanu El in 1915.

Tucson has always had a strong Jewish community. Temple Emmanu El was the city's first synagogue. The building was completed in 1910 at a cost of $10,000, all from pledges and private donations. Worship continued at the site until 1949 when it closed. The original building, which is located at 564 South Stone Avenue, is a designated historic site.

Temple Emmanu El congregation has been at 225 North Country Club Road since its move in 1949.

LABOR STRIKE

Tucson has never been much of a union town so it was downright shocking when transit drivers parked their buses and walked off the job in 1918.

The strike began August 15, 1918, and was about money. Most transit drivers at the time earned about twenty-three cents per hour. After three days of picketing, the Tucson Rapid Transit Company agreed to raise the wages of its drivers by just over three cents per hour. The offer was accepted and the drivers returned to work

LAMPLIGHTER

During a brief period of experimentation, Tucson flirted with the concept of gaslights. Several dozen of the flickering lamps were installed near the old courthouse. The Tucson Gas Company hired Clyde James to light the lamps each evening at dusk. James was not married and lived in a small apartment at the gas works.

LAUNDRY

The first public laundry in Tucson was actually an irrigation ditch near Pearl Street.

The ditch wasn't just a place to wash clothes. It was also a popular gathering place and even served as a public bathing area. After washing clothes, most people jumped in the ditch to bathe.

The irrigation ditch was also where people celebrated San Juan's feast day. People from throughout the area gathered each June 24th near the ditch to picnic, enjoy music and perhaps even a cockfight.

In 1871, a commercial laundry business opened by a Chinese family on Main Street near Pearl Street.

LIBRARY

Jacob Mansfield loved books.

In 1870, he opened the Pioneer News Depot and Bookstore. It was the first book store in Arizona. In addition to the latest novels by Eggleston and James, Mansfield also sold newspapers from outside the area. In 1871, he started a small lending library in his shop.

During the 1880s, Mansfield worked to establish a public library in Tucson. A city ordinance passed

The Carnegie Library in about 1915.

in 1883 was the first crucial step. Space was found on the second floor of the old city hall building and after several months, the library was opened to the public. The original collection was only several dozen books but quickly expanded to over 700 volumes, mostly books that had been donated. Mansfield served as the library's first trustee.

The first building constructed exclusively as a library was the Carnegie Library on Sixth Avenue

72

between East 12th and East 13th Streets. The structure was designed in the French Renaissance style and trimmed in terra cotta and cast stone. The architect was H.C. Trost. The new library opened in 1900 and even featured an outdoor patio area for its patrons.

An ad for Jacob Mansfeld's Bookstore in 1882.

LOTTERY

The first Tucson lottery was not a success. In January of 1869, Francis Hodges announced a raffle in the Weekly Arizonan. The prize was his hotel. Hodges House consisted of twelve large rooms, several outbuildings and a garden on about a half acre. Three hundred and fifty tickets were being offered at $20 per crack. A special committee was set up to make certain the lottery drawing was

73

honest. No winner was ever announced which indicates the tickets failed to sell.

An attempt was made a decade later to establish a statewide lottery.

John C. Fremont was elected the fifth Territorial governor in 1878. Hopes were high he would help Tucson since he maintained a home here. Instead of helping his neighbors in the Old Pueblo, Fremont devoted most of his time and energy planning a lottery bill that he hoped would raise much needed cash to help finance the Territorial government. The bill was passed by the Territorial Legislature but later vetoed by the U.S. Congress.

LYNCHING

During the summer of 1873, a crime occurred in Tucson that was so brutal, it triggered a public lynching.

Vincente and Librada Hernandez owned a small shop near the corner of Meyer and Kennedy Streets. They closed the afternoon of August 6, 1873, because of the heat. Even after the sun had set, it was still hot and stuffy. Vincente and his wife decided to bed down near the front door of the shop in an attempt to enjoy what little air might be stirring. The next morning they were found slaughtered in their makeshift bed.

Vincente had a crushed skull and a body punctured with 17 knife wounds. His wife had also been beaten and stabbed to death. Even in a town that was still rough around the edges, the Hernandez murders were especially vicious.

A group of businessmen led by William Zeckendorf quickly sealed off all roads leading out of town.

The crime was solved following a tip. A neighbor of Jesus Zaguarita saw the man stumble home the night before covered with blood. He reported what he had seen to Sheriff W.S. Oury. An armed posse found Zaguarita still asleep at his home. When loot was found which had come from the murder scene, Zaguarita quickly confessed. He implicated two friends, Leonardo Cordoba and Clemente Lopez. His two accomplices were rounded up and the three men jailed.

The next morning, people were filled with both sorrow and anger. As a funeral mass was being conducted for Mr. and Mrs. Hernandez, a group gathered in front of the courthouse. By noon, the crowd had swelled to over 2,000 people. Zeckendorf and several other members of the self-appointed "Committee of Safety" stormed the jail. They seized the three suspected of the Hernandez killings and a fourth prisoner, John Willis, who was also awaiting trial for murder. The four men were quickly lynched, despite protests of former Marshal Milton Duffield.

McDONALD'S

When the first McDonald's Restaurant opened in Tucson in 1961, a cheeseburger, fries and a soft drink sold for less than fifty cents.

Cheeseburgers were priced at twenty cents each, fries ten cents and a beverage -- soft drinks, milk or coffee -- also ten cents.

The first McDonald's Restaurant opened September 19, 1961, and was located at 5351 East Speedway Blvd.

MARSHAL

William Morgan was hired as the first town marshal when Tucson incorporated in 1871.

He was paid $20 per month and for that princely sum he was expected to run the jail, care for all city prisoners, keep the streets free of all trash and litter, collect taxes, control stray animals and quell all criminal activities within the town limits.

It's no wonder that in less than three months, Morgan quit and cleared out of town

MASCOT

Wilbur the Wildcat, the official mascot of the University of Arizona, made his first appearance at the University of Arizona-Texas game, November 7, 1959.

The Masonic Lodge in 1918.

MASONIC LODGE

Jacob Mansfield was a pioneer businessman who helped found the town's first public library. He also was one of the earliest supporters of building the University of Arizona in Tucson. Throughout the 1880s, he was a major mover and shaker.

One October evening in 1881, Jacobs invited a few friends to his home on Church Street. Together they signed a charter granted by the M.W. Grant Lodge of California establishing the

76

first Masonic Lodge in Tucson. It was designated Lodge #4 on the roll of Arizona lodges.

MATERNITY HOSPITAL

The Stork's Nest was Tucson's first facility that specialized in the birth of babies.

It opened its doors in 1922 by Mrs. Helen V. Jacobs in a building on North Court Avenue. The maternity home had ten rooms that rented during the 1930s for  about $25 per day. The average stay for a new mother at the Stork's Nest was about a week.

The Stork's Nest closed in 1946 following the death of Mrs. Jacobs.

Sidney R. DeLong, Tucson's mayor in 1871.

MAYOR

Jose Leon was the first civilian mayor of Tucson. He was appointed January 1, 1825, when less than 400 people lived within the immediate area of the Presidio.

When the town incorporated in 1871, Sidney R. DeLong served as the first mayor to be elected. Other officials in DeLong's administration included Hiram Stevens, treasurer, and W.J. Osborn, assessor and recorder. The four councilmen were Sam Hughes,

W.W. Williams, Charles O. Brown and William S. Oury.

DeLong, who had been a soldier, scholar and merchant, died in a rooming house on North Stone Avenue in 1914, at the age of 85. Although he had made several fortunes during his lifetime, at the time of his death he was broke and forgotten.

MEXICAN SOCIAL CLUB

Although several Hispanic organizations flourished in Tucson during the 1870s, the first Mexican-American group of real consequence was the Una Patriotica Mexicans that met as early as 1885. The group was primarily social in nature.

In 1896, the Alianza Hispano-Americans formed following a meeting at the print shop of Carlos Velasco. Velasco was the editor-publisher of El Fonterizo, an important Hispanic newspaper that was published on West Cushing Street. Velasco campaigned, both in his newspaper and through his newly formed political action group, for repatriation to Mexico. His newspaper ceased publication in about 1914.

Alianza Hispano-Americans continued as an organization, however. By 1930, there were 240 chapters in six western states and Mexico. At its peak, the organization claimed over 20,000 members.

MILITARY POST - U.S.

U.S. solders were stationed in Tucson as early as 1862, when a post was established near the center of town. The primitive post was abandoned during the autumn of 1864. Following the end of the Civil War, the post was once again activated. Camp Lowell, named for Brigadier General Charles Lowell, killed during a Civil War battle in Virginia, quickly expanded to include over 100 military personnel and about 350 acres both east and south of the city center.

Ruins of Fort Lowell, Tucson, Ariz.

The ruins of Fort Lowell in 1915.

Camp Lowell was moved in 1872 when General George Crook observed that the old site was "unfit for the occupation of animals, much less the troops of a civilized nation." Being so close to the town center was also considered too much of a temptation for the soldiers stationed at the facility. A new post was established just northeast of town near present day Craycroft Road.

Fort Lowell served as the headquarters of the Sixth U.S. Cavalry and was finally closed in 1891.

Ruins at the site include the adobe foundation and walls of what is left of an Army hospital where Walter Reed practiced between 1876 and 1877.

MILITIA

As street crime continued to soar, several Tucson citizens met in 1875 to confront the problem. The Arizona Minute Men was formed with R.N. Leatherwood, a former Confederate soldier and owner of stables at the corner of Pennington and Church, president of the group.

The purpose of the Arizona Minute Men was simple. The members saw that much of Tucson's crime problem had to do with being close to the international border. The group's stated purpose was "to aid the enforcement of the law, to give peace to the people of both sides of the line, and help to put down the thieves and murderers who infest the border and commit crimes in Sonora and flee to Arizona for safety, then repeat their crime in Arizona and escape to Sonora."

Soon after the formation of the militia, George Buttner was elected town marshal.

MOVIE

The first motion picture shown in Tucson was under the stars at Elysian Grove.

Although the first demonstration of motion pictures in Arizona was probably in about 1901 at

Globe, Arizona, Emanuel Drachman introduced films here in 1903.

He built a small screen in the park, set up a primitive hand-cranked projector and one evening in 1903 the images of "The Great Train Robbery" flickered into view. The movies in the park were so successful, Drachman installed a projector and screen in the  Opera House where films could be shown to much larger audiences. Films at the Opera House were being advertised as early as 1905.

MOVIE PREMIERE

Tucson had never seen anything quite like it. The town was crawling with celebrities and it was all because of a movie.

The excitement began in 1939 when scouts from Hollywood arrived in town to check out possible locations for a new film that promised to be a major hit. During the spring of 1940, a small army of several hundred workers began building a movie set just west of town. The set would duplicate the Tucson of the 1860s. Shooting began that June.

A set built at "Old Tucson" for the 1940 film.

*A scene from
"Arizona".*

"Arizona" featured two of Hollywood's biggest stars -- William Holden and Jean Arthur.

By the night of the premiere, excitement was at a fever pitch. The film debuted the evening of November 14, 1940, at a glittering premiere at the Temple of Art and Music. Network radio broadcasts from the Pioneer Hotel described the parades, street dances and the celebrating downtown. Without a doubt, it was one of the biggest parties ever thrown in these parts.

The movie set which had been built for the production was saved. It was used for other movie and television productions. By the 1950s, "Old Tucson" had become a major tourist attraction and remains one to this day.

MOVIE PROJECTOR

The first movie projector in Arizona was one demonstrated in Globe in about 1901. Emanuel Drachman set up a projector in Eylsian Grove in Tucson in 1903 for a special showing of "The Great

Train Robbery." It is rather appropriate that the first movie shown in southern Arizona was a western.

MOVIE-SOUND

The first all-talkie feature length film shown in Tucson was also a western. "In Old Arizona," which had been partially shot on location near Tucson, opened at the Rialto Theatre in March of 1929.

Roy Drachman, who was manager of the Rialto, predicted talkies would usher in a new era of entertainment in southern Arizona. For the first time, he said, audiences in Tucson would be able to see -- and hear -- such outstanding performers as Al Jolson and Fanny Brice. Admission for "In Old Arizona" was sixty cents for seats on the lower floor and forty cents for those in the balcony.

"In Old Arizona" was followed at the Rialto by Charles King in "Broadway Melody," the first musical to win an Oscar, "Singing Fool" with Al Jolson and "The Canary Murder Case" starring William Powell as ace detective Philo Vance.

MOVIE SOUND EFFECTS

The first films were silent. To make them more exciting, Julius Bookman was hired by theatre manager Joe R. Scotti. As films were being projected on the screen, Bookman stood off stage providing the sound effects that often included pistol shots, automobile horns, thunder and even howling wind.

The system was simple. Bookman watched each film and then planned his effects. His timing had to be perfect to be effective. The gimmick was a big success, both for Bookman and his boss, Joe Scott.

MOVIE - 3-D

In February of 1953, large splashy ads in the Tucson newspapers announced a gimmick that Hollywood hoped would save movies from that evil monster called television. It was a process called three dimensional or 3-D. Two cameras were used to shoot the action. When special glasses were worn to view the film, the screen appeared to have depth.

The newspaper campaign worked. Long lines snaked down the block in front of the Paramount Theatre on East Congress Street the morning of February 27, 1953, as tickets went on sale.

Posters outside the theatre were lurid. "Bwana Devil" didn't have much of a plot. Railroad workers in Africa tried to keep a step or two ahead of hungry lions as Robert Stack and Barbara Britton fought to keep the railroad running and, between animal attacks, find time for an occasional clinch or two in the jungle. Who cared about plot when lions seemed to jump right off the screen?

Admission for "Bwana Devil" was $1.15 weekend evenings. Balcony seating was 90 cents. Each showing of the limited engagement was a sell-out. Despite the box office magic of 3-D films, enthusiasm soon faded. It had been nothing more than a passing fad.

MOVIES AT NIGHT

Before the 1920s, the streets of downtown Tucson were usually deserted by eight 'clock each evening. Movie theatres emptied after the six o'clock feature and even the drug stores promptly closed shortly after dark.

Stone Avenue at night, circa 1940.

Empty theaters didn't make money and that bothered Joe R. Scotti. Scotti leased a downtown theatre and he came up with an idea that changed the early to bed sleeping patterns of many of the people who lived in Tucson.

85

When Scotti announced that he planned to show late evening films at his theater, some predicted failure. Scotti wasn't completely convinced it would work himself and covered his bet by offering free door prizes of dishes and gasoline. When people realized there was action downtown at night, the business district suddenly came alive after dark. Film lovers enjoyed attending movies at night and, perhaps, a quick, chocolate sundae at George Martin's Drug Store down the street. With increased foot traffic at night, many stores -- including the drug stores -- remained open until nine o'clock, all because of an idea of a theatre manager.

MUNICIPAL AIRPORT

The Tucson Municipal Airport in 1928.

Tucson's municipal airport came about because of an undertaker who was fascinated by airplanes.

O.C. Parker was a funeral director and when he was elected mayor in 1916, one of his first goals was to establish a municipal airport.

In 1919, a plot of flat land was purchased on South Sixth Avenue, now the site of the Rodeo arena. The site, considered ideal by Billy Mitchell acting on behalf of the U.S. War Department, was quickly developed. With mule power, a runway was constructed and an old WWI hanger moved from Nogales. After a total expenditure of $5,000, Tucson opened the first municipally owned airport in the United States.

In 1927, the airport was moved just east of the Southern Pacific Railroad tracks and re-named

Davis-Monthan Field. Flying Ace Charles Lindbergh dedicated the new field in 1928.

Standard Airlines, which later became American Airlines, began service at the new airport in 1928. That same year runway lights were installed making Tucson's Municipal Airport the first in the nation to offer night flights on a regular schedule.

NATIONAL ASSOCIATION FOR THE ADVANCEMENT OF COLORED PEOPLE

Creed Taylor was a leader in the black community of Tucson. He was responsible for establishing the first local chapter of the National Association for the Advancement of Colored People

(NAACP). The year was 1918.

In 1926, he was named chief engineer of the Desert Sanitarium, now known as the Tucson Medical Center.

The Tucson Medical Center in 1948.

NEWSBOYS

Monte Manfield and his friend, Roy Seeley, were the first newsboys to hawk papers on the downtown street corners of Tucson.

87

They began selling copies of the Arizona Star in about 1896. Monte, who was twelve, was the son of Jacob Mansfield, a political leader who was responsible for establishing the first public library in the Old Pueblo. The sales skills, which Monte and Roy perfected as youngsters, came in handy for them later as adults. Monte Manfield opened the first Ford dealership in Tucson in 1914. Roy Seeley was a successful realtor in Los Angeles.

NEWSPAPER

The first newspaper published in Arizona was the Weekly Arizonan, printed in Tubac on a hand-press March 3, 1859.

The newspaper changed ownership and was moved to Tucson that same summer. The first issue published in Tucson by J. Howard Wells hit the streets August 4, 1859. Subscription rates for the Weekly Arizonan was three dollars per year, in advance.

The front-page news featured in the first Tucson edition reported the great mineral strikes in the Rocky Mountains and the abundance of coal in the United States. Local news was scanty.

An ad promoting The Arizona Daily Star circa 1895.

NEWSPAPER - DAILY

The first issue of the Arizona Citizen was published the afternoon of Saturday, October 15, 1870. It wasn't exactly an exciting issue. In addition to ads, the main story in the four-page paper was about the theft of mules and a horse that had been stolen that week from a ranch just outside of town.

From that rather modest beginning, the weekly publication eventually evolved into the Tucson Daily Citizen, Arizona's oldest continuously published newspaper.

Journalism in Tucson in 1885.

Tucson's first daily newspaper lasted less than six months. Publisher Louis Hughes had high hopes for the Tucson Bulletin in 1877 but the paper failed to survive. Hughes made a second attempt two years later when he launched the Daily Star in January of 1879. This time he was successful. The Daily Star was the first daily paper to survive in Tucson. Pioneer Publisher John Clum met the

90

challenge of the Daily Star when he converted the Citizen to a daily publication several weeks following the actions of the Daily Star. John Clum founded the Tombstone Epitaph in 1880. He published the Tombstone paper until 1883 when it was sold.

OPERA HOUSE

Tucson was giddy with excitement.

The great Sarah Bernhardt was coming to town. Not only that, she was coming with five carloads of scenery, costumes, props and 40 players for a one-night-only production of "Camille" at Tucson's Opera House.

A Tucson parade in 1887, showing both the Opera House and the Courthouse.

The excitement had reached a peak by the evening of April 17, 1911. It was a defining moment for the Opera House. Bernhardt was greeted by an ovation when she walked onto the stage. She emoted and

91

swooned through the production. It was an unforgettable evening.

While the magic still lingered in the air, the Divine Sarah climbed aboard the train early the next morning, off to conquer other hearts elsewhere.

The Tucson Opera House was the first theatre in town built to accommodate Grand Opera. It was designed by A.V. Grossetta and constructed on the north side of Congress Street between Stone Avenue and Sixth. The main entrance was through a passageway from Congress Street.

The Opera House opened November 11, 1897, with a lavish production of "La Mascota" featuring the Grauy Opera Company. During its glittering history, its stage was graced by some of the best performers ever including James K. Hackett, Minnie Maddern Fiske and Nat Goodwin.

In 1918, a fire damaged the grand old theatre and when it re-opened several months later, the stage was smaller and gone, too, were its glory days. The Opera House hosted vaudeville acts, was later named The State Theater when it became a movie house. The theatre was finally demolished during the autumn of 1953. The final movie shown was "Red Mountain" starring Alan Ladd.

OPIUM DENS

Opium dens were clearly shown on city maps during the 1880s. Most were along Pearl Street near North Street. The Chinese were in Tucson following the construction work of the railroad and the dens were popular throughout the 1880s and 90s. Some were even operating as late as 1910 just west of city hall.

PARK

Leopoldo Carrillo was a man with a vision.

He saw a patch of eight acres on South Main Street and set out to create an urban oasis. Large cottonwood trees provided inviting shade and flowerbeds graced an area near several natural springs.

The park eventually featured a saloon for the thirsty, ice cream for the hungry and a dance hall for the bored. With the money he made from the park, Carrillo wisely invested in Tucson real estate. When he died in 1890, he was one of the most successful businessmen in town.

Warm, dry *Sunshine* now ‥ in
TUCSON

PARKING METERS

In 1939, the Tucson City Council ordered the installation of parking meters for the downtown business district. After the announcement, all hell broke loose.

Just the thought of those pesky parking meters made people livid. So livid, they unleashed their wrath during several council sessions and the plan quietly shelved.

In 1952, Mayor Ben Emery decided the time might be right and he cautiously ordered about a dozen of the meters for installation near City Hall. Although people still grumbled, they didn't storm City Hall as they had twelve years earlier. Within a year, over 100 meters were happily gobbling

Bystanders look glum as first parking meters are installed in Tucson in 1952.

pennies and nickels along the streets of downtown Tucson.

PHOTOGRAPHER

J.C. Gaige stepped off the stage in Tucson one afternoon in 1868. His baggage included several crude cameras. The Santa Fe man was hired by the Weekly Arizonan and he probably was the first professional photographer to work in Tucson.

One of the earliest surviving photographs of the Old Pueblo is a bird's eye view from Sentinel Peak taken by Henry Watkins in about 1880.

Carlton Waltkins traveled throughout Arizona during the 1880s and captured some of the first stereographic views of the area.

95

PHOTOGRAPHY STUDIO

Henry Buehman opened a professional portrait gallery during the summer of 1874. He advertised himself as both a dentist and photographer. It didn't take Buehman long to discover that he enjoyed snapping the shutters of a camera much more than the pulling of teeth.

Buehman quickly established a reputation for being one of the best photographers in the area. His first studio was on the corner of Court House and Maiden Lane. He next moved to a small studio on Congress Street and in 1881 built a two-story studio further east. It was one of the best photography studios in southern Arizona and featured a skylight and the very latest equipment available.

PHYSICAN

Tucson got its first doctor because of a bribe.

John C. Handy was brilliant. He had graduated from Cooper Medical College when he was barely 19. He later served as an army surgeon in California and as a contract surgeon at several military camps including Camp Grant and Camp Goodwin in Arizona. By the time he arrived in Tucson, his medical reputation had been well established.

Dr. Handy shortly before he was killed on the streets of Tucson.

Sam Hughes was a crusty old pioneer who suffered from chronic lung problems. He met and was impressed by Dr. Handy. Hughes asked the doctor if he would consider setting up a practice in Tucson. The town needed a good doctor. Dr. Handy said he would only if he could be guaranteed an income of at least $2,500 a year. Hughes contacted several friends and soon raised the money. Tucson had its first certified medical doctor.

The Tucson City Director of 1881 lists Dr. Handy as both physician and city health officer.

During the summer of 1891, Dr. Handy was involved in a messy divorce. His wife, who had a drug problem, retained Francis Heney as her attorney. Dr. Handy was livid with anger. That September, Dr. Handy came face to face with Heney on the corner of Pennington and Church Street. An argument erupted and insults exchanged. The doctor struck Heney across the face with his hand. The attorney then pulled a gun. There was a struggle, the gun exploded and Dr. Handy fell to the sidewalk wounded by a bullet that had ripped through his abdomen. Dr. Handy died several hours later at his home.

Although Heney was charged with murder, he was exonerated when he testified that Dr. Handy had tried to run him down with his buggy several days before the shooting.

PIANO

Musical instruments were mainly limited to violins and guitars during the early 1860s in Tucson.

Charles Brown, the owner of the Congress Hall Saloon, created great excitement when he announced in 1869 that he had ordered a piano for his wife, Clara.

Not just any piano but a genuine Steinway square grand.

The piano arrived months later by wagon. It had been shipped from St. Louis. It was delivered to the Brown home at 40 West Broadway. People from throughout the area came to gawk at the wonderful instrument, the first ever seen in Arizona.

POLICE CHIEF

In 1881, A.G. Buttner was appointed Tucson's Chief of Police following an all day celebration at Levin's Park.

Buttner was a busy man if the arrest records of November 1882 are typical. During that one month, Chief Buttner made 79 arrests. Six men were arrested for being drunk; 37 for vagrancy; 13 for assault; two for burglary; two for petit larceny; one each for firing a gun within the city limits, disturbing the peace, attempted murder and grand larceny; and even a cowboy arrested for racing his horse downtown. Sixty-five of the prisoners were Anglo, the others Hispanic or Indian.

On May 8, 1883, the Tucson Police Department was officially formed. Chief Buttner received a salary of $120 a month and had six officers under his command to maintain order in the town. Tucson boasted a population of about 7,000 people during the early 1880s.

Chief A.G. Buttner

100

POLICE - MOTORCYCLE OFFICER

Jack Anderson was a motorcycle officer for the Tucson Police Department. Records are sketchy about when he began with the department but some sources suggest he served as early as 1910.

The Tucson Police Department in about 1930 including motorcycle patrolmen and the only female police officer.

His motorcycle was a twin-cylinder Thor that had a tendency to overheat. Sometimes while in pursuit of a speeding motorist, Anderson would look down and see his leather puttees smoking from the heat of the bike's engine. The chase would then have to be called off.

POLICE OFFICER - FEMALE

Nora Sullivan was the daughter of a Fort Lowell Quartermaster Sergeant. She was a determined young woman who wanted to be a Tucson police officer. She married William Nugent, a railroad man, and for a short time operated a small café on Congress Street.

Nora Sullivan got her big chance in 1929. She was hired by the Tucson Police Department and continued as its first and only female officer until 1933, when her job was eliminated by the city council. The department would not hire another female officer until 1952.

POLICE OFFICER KILLED IN THE LINE OF DUTY

Officer William Elliott was patrolling Meyer Street the night of July 2, 1892. While on foot patrol, he saw Santos Alvarado, a known felon. Alvarado was drunk.

When the officer attempted an arrest, Alvarado lunged at Elliot with a knife. It was over in an instant. William Elliott fell to the sidewalk bleeding to death. The officer was survived by his wife and had three small children.

POLICE - RADIO CAR

In 1939, the Tucson Police Department unveiled the latest in crime fighting equipment -- radio cars.

The first official transmission occurred the evening of May 29, 1939, when Officer Oliver White sent a radio message to Car 29 requesting that Officers Baker Hardin and Ellmont Saylor investigate a report of motorcyclists racing near Tyndall and 7th Street.

POLICE - TRUANT OFFICER

A.M. "Jake" Meyer was a kid's worst nightmare.

Mose Drachman was a Tucson school board member who was concerned about truancy. In 1922, he and other members of the board recruited Meyer as the town's first truant officer.

Meyer patrolled downtown movie theatres, parks and ice cream parlors in search of students who were skipping classes. He was good at his work. School attendance took a dramatic jump, from 74% when he began in 1922, to an astonishing 97% the following year. Meyer served as truant officer until his retirement in 1952.

POPULATION

In 1821, one of the first official counts found 395 people living in what is now Tucson. Most of those counted were soldiers who were assigned to the Presidio.

The official nose count of 1831 found a slight increase, a population of 465. U.S. Marshal Milton B. Duffield counted 1,568 people here in 1864.

U.S. Marshal Milton B. Duffield

103

POSTMASTER

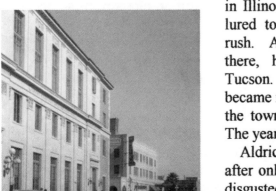

The Tucson Post Office during the 1940s.

Mark Aldrich deserted his wife and six children in Illinois in 1850 when he was lured to California by the gold rush. After spending five years there, he backtracked east to Tucson. He opened a small store, became mayor and was appointed the town's first U.S. Postmaster. The year was 1865.

Aldrich quit his postal work after only three months. He was disgusted by the fact that he was rarely paid.

The rather sour, grim-faced man next turned his attention to Tucson crime. As a judge, he erected a whipping post on the town's plaza. A prisoner found guilty was often sentenced to 20 lashes. After ten were given, the prisoner was released and told to report the next day for the rest of his punishment. More likely than not, the culprit would not stick around for more lashes. He would high tail it out of town. Some people liked Aldrich better when he had served as

Mark Aldrich.

postmaster. After he became a judge, he got downright mean.

Aldrich abruptly quit the bench in disgust when he witnessed a murder in downtown Tucson. He issued a statement. "Yesterday, a man was shot dead in the street, in open daylight, in the presence of a number of witnesses," his angry letter began. It continued "not a word is said about arresting the person who committed the deed or seeing the laws are enforced." He was livid and threw in the towel.

Having a wife and family in Illinois did not prevent Aldrich from starting a second family in Arizona. He lived with a Hispanic woman named Leon and together they had a daughter, Faustina. Aldrich died in 1873, probably scowling to the bitter end.

PRESBYTERIAN CHURCH

A brief announcement in the April 4, 1876, issue of the Tucson Citizen said that Presbyterian worship services would be conducted at the courthouse that Sunday. As an extra enticement for the men, the article further reported "the ladies will certainly be there. They are always forward in every good work and deed."

That first service was one that was conducted by Reverend Jackson. By the following autumn, Reverend J.E. Anderson had arrived and he found a small lot just west of the town's plaza. The first Presbyterian Church was completed there in 1878. It was also the first church constructed in Tucson, exclusively for Protestant worship. The congregation struggled for over a decade before the $6,000 building debt was finally retired. The original Presbyterian Church was demolished in

1917, following extensive commercial development in the downtown district.

PRESIDENTIAL VISITS

Rutherford B. Hayes was the first U.S. President to visit Tucson while in office. The Presidential visit was prompted by the arrival of the Southern Pacific Railroad to the Old Pueblo in 1880.

The President arrived and was greeted by Mayor Robert Leatherwood and numerous other town leaders including W.W. Williams. Williams was a partner in the mercantile company of Lord and Williams and he lived in one of the most impressive houses in town. President Hayes was escorted to the Williams home and after a brief rest, he began shaking hands and greeting the hundreds of people who arrived at the mansion to see a genuine American President on the hoof.

Ironically, the arrival of the railroad brought ruin to Williams in less than a year. Following the collapse of his business, he fled to Mexico where he died in 1884. He spent his last years trying to convince insurance companies he was dead so he could collect on his policies.

Other Presidential visits to Tucson include Benjamin Harrison who campaigned from the train in 1888 and William McKinley who arrived with his wife in 1901. Herbert Hoover spoke in Tucson during his unsuccessful re-election campaign of 1932.

Theodore Roosevelt, the leader of the Rough Riders, visited Tucson in 1912, following his term in Washington. Before leaving Arizona, Teddy also made a short trip to see the Grand Canyon, which he no doubt thought was bully.

PROPERTY TAXES

Property taxes have always been hated in Tucson. In 1873, when the city incorporated, money was needed to finance the running of the town's government. Property taxes was the solution but the taxes were easier to establish than collect.

When property owners balked, the city sweetened the deal. Anyone paying four dollars or more in property taxes could -- are you ready for this -- claim a free building lot within the city limits. The offer was so attractive some even tried to pay taxes where none was owed. Over $4,000 in tax revenues was raised that first year.

PROSTITUTE

The first prostitutes in Tucson were -- no doubt -- on the scene within a day or two of the soldiers when the construction began on the Presidio.

One of the first people to actually record his personal dealings with prostitutes here was George Hand, a Tucson saloon owner. During the 1870s after an hour or so with one of the soiled doves of Tucson, Hand recorded the event in his diary. Hand visited Maiden Lane, Tucson's red light district, frequently to share moments of joy with Refugia, Louise and Juana. Even moments of joy came at a price, however, and that price during the 1870s was usually a dollar or two.

In 1910, Tucson began the regulation of prostitution. A city medical officer examined each of the women on a monthly basis and if found to be free of disease, she was given what amounted to a work permit. The price of the exam was a dollar, the work permit five dollars. Both had to be renewed every 30 days.

Myrtle.

Bessie.

Molly.

Three "soiled doves"
of Tucson in about
1910.

In 1910, a registration of prostitutes working the cribs of Tucson listed some 69 women including Belgian Annie, Toughluck from Phoenix, French Jennie, Gold Tooth and Juliette Mays, who was also identified as "Butch's girl."

CITY OF TUCSON
HEALTH DEPARTMENT

Tucson, Arizona, 10 - 28 191___

THIS CERTIFIES that I have this day Examined Lizzie Parker

who lives at No. 12 - _____St., Tucson, Ariz., and find her free

from any contagious disease. This Certificate is good until_____191___

Done in pursuance of provisions of Ordinance No. 48.

Countersigned:_____

_____City Recorder.

Health Officer.

CITY OF TUCSON
HEALTH DEPARTMENT

Tucson, Arizona, 10 - 21 191___

THIS CERTIFIES that I have this day examined Loraine Wear

who lives at No. 6 - 12 - _____St., Tucson, Ariz., and find her free

from any contagious disease. This certificate is good until_____191___

Done in pursuance of provisions of Ordinance No. 48.

Countersigned:_____

_____City Recorder.

Health Office

"Work permits" issued in the
Red Light District by the City of
Tucson.

PSYCHIATRIST

Dr. Lindsay E. Beaton, M.D., was born in Chicago. He received his medical training at Northwestern University School of Medicine.

During WWII, Dr. Beaton served as an Lt. Colonel in the Medical Corps of the U.S. Army. He was clinical Director of Psychiatry for the 10th Army and a member of the Pacific Ocean Area's Psychiatry team.

He established a practice in Tucson following the war, becoming the town's first psychiatrist. He served as president of the Arizona Medical Association in 1960. Dr. Beaton died in 1967.

PUBLIC TRANSPORTATION

During the 1880s, Tucson's public transportation often came to a grinding halt when the mule sat down to rest.

In 1879, Tucson's public transportation system consisted of a mule, a small cart and a man who saw a need. Bill Morgan made the daily run from town to the Nine Mile watering hole, just northwest of town on the Santa Cruz River. He would meet the incoming stage.

When the Southern Pacific Railroad chugged into town in 1880, he expanded his route to include the depot.

Although there were earlier transportation systems, one of the first to publish and maintain a regular schedule was the University Hack line which began operations in 1893.

Mules continued to toil on the streetcar routes until 1906 when animal power was replaced by the more dependable electric trolleys. The streetcar lines were abandoned in 1930. Many of the original tracks still remain buried under many of Tucson's downtown streets.

In June of 1926, the Tucson Citizen hired an Albuquerque engineer to install a radio transmitter on the roof of the newspaper building on Stone Avenue at Jackson. J.F. Walsh, the engineer, erected a small tower and began transmitting sound tones and patterns three times each week.

While Walsh was sending tones, KGAR Radio signed on the air June 10, 1926. After a short announcement, George Chambers played music on a Victrola throughout that first day. The small studio was on Stone Avenue. Tucson's first radio station, which has always been at 1400 on the AM dial, eventually changed its call-letters to KTUC-AM.

RADIO - BLACK PROGRAMMING

In 1948, KCNA-AM tried an experiment. James Brownlow was hired to host a weekend program that included news from the black community of Tucson and a mixture of both gospel and jazz music. Brownlow was the city's first black radio host.

RADIO - FEMALE ANNOUNCER

It took a world war and a manpower shortage to finally get a female announcer on Tucson radio.

In 1944, the shortage of male announcers was critical and the time had come to try something new. Patricia Perley had a crisp, clear voice and she auditioned for Ben Slack, the program director of KVOA-AM. She was hired to do station identification breaks throughout the afternoon during the NBC line-up of soap operas.

Cele Peterson also was a female radio pioneer. She hosted a fashion broadcast each Saturday morning, heard on KVOA-AM. The program originated from Cele Peterson's dress shop on East Pennington and was probably the first remote, scheduled on a regular basis, and hosted by a woman.

RADIO-FM

Tom Wallace loved classical music. He was responsible for getting Tucson's first FM radio station on the air, KTKT-FM (99.5). Wallace hired

Jack Frakes, a drama teacher at Rincon High School, as his announcer.

In 1959, Wallace concocted a way to broadcast in stereo but listeners had to have two radios to hear it. Each Sunday afternoon at two o'clock, Wallace transmitted two separate radio signals, one on the AM band and the other on the FM. It was tricky and far from perfect but with two radios tuned just

right, listeners could hear something approaching stereophonic sound. In 1960, KTKT-FM was purchased by Lee Little in and the call letters were changed to KFMM-FM.

RADIO NETWORK

The first radio network in Arizona began during the 1930s. The Arizona Broadcasting Company was the brainchild of the management of KTAR-AM radio in Phoenix. News programs and entertainment segments were produced for the radio stations of Yuma, Safford, Douglas, Globe, Prescott and KVOA-AM in Tucson. Howard Pyle, the program director of KTAR, hosted "Arizona

Highlights," a folksy program that spotlighted the people and places of Arizona.

To prevent confusion, KTAR changed the name of the Arizona Broadcasting Company to the Arizona Broadcasting System when the national network of the American Broadcasting Company was formed. KTAR's call letters reflected its original ownership by The Arizona Republic newspaper in Phoenix.

RADIO - PROMOTION

Although there were many goofy radio promotions in Tucson during the 1930s, one was a standout in every respect.

In 1939, KVOA-AM radio moved to its new digs on East Broadway. It decided to celebrate the event by hatching up what become known as the big ice melt.

KVOA issued a challenge to radio stations in KUMA in Yuma and KTAR in Phoenix. Large

cakes of ice were delivered to each station and the ice melt derby began. Throughout that hot August day, progress reports were broadcast, the ice measured. Ben Slack, the program director of KVOA, walked around in snowshoes and blizzard gear as he examined the ice in front of his building. Listeners loved it and even claimed they felt cooler just hearing the ice melt reports and the sound effects of howling, winter winds. KVOA even featured an interview with two arctic explorers. After a full day of fun and foolishness, the ice in both Yuma and Phoenix was gone. Tucson had won the ice melt contest and everyone called the promotion a bracing success.

RADIO - SPORTS ANNOUNCER

Jim Officer began broadcasting the University of Arizona football games on radio during the 1930s. He was probably the first sports announcer in Tucson. His friend, Bill Rider, often called the play-by-play.

RADIO - TRANSMISSION

Max P. Vosskuhler and his friend, Dr. Paul Cloke, built a crude 50-watt transmitter at the University of Arizona. That August, Dean G.M. Butler requested $500 to erect a 150-foot steel tower. It was constructed in 1923, mainly through the efforts of student volunteers. Operating on 360 meters, the station began broadcasts in March of 1923. The early programming included music, sports and limited news. The great radio experiment came to a halt after about a month. The station ended because of a lack of funding. The University of Arizona would not establish another radio station until 1939.

RAILROAD

It was one of the biggest parties ever hosted by the City of Tucson. The railroad was finally coming to town.

In March of 1880, businessmen decorated the

The Southern Pacific Depot in 1948.

front of their commercial buildings with red, white and blue bunting. The band of the Sixth Cavalry of Fort Lowell provided military marches and pomp. Every available rooming house and hotel were filled to capacity with people who wanted to celebrate the event.

Hundreds of people crowded around the depot as the first train huffed into town. After a few speeches, everyone adjourned to Levin's Park where serious drinking and celebrating were soon underway.

The original wooden railway station, completed in February of 1880, was destroyed by fire in 1907. It was then replaced by a more permanent structure.

The railroad yard near the station was the scene of one of Tucson's most famous shoot-outs. In March of 1882, Wyatt Earp tracked Frank Stillwell there and killed him. Earp suspected Stillwell of murdering his brother, Morgan, earlier in Tombstone. The Tucson shooting had been one of revenge.

REAL ESTATE DEVELOPER

There were earlier real estate developers before John Murphey, but no one who had the style and vision that he did.

John, and his wife Helen, began their married life in a tent pitched near the present intersection of North Campbell Avenue and East River Road. They lived in the tent until their homestead claim on 640 acres there was established. During the 1920s, the first Catalina Foothills Estates homes were built. They established some of the earliest covenants ever in the city to protect their developed properties.

A bird's eye view of Tucson from the 1930s.

The Murpheys soon joined efforts with Swiss architect Josias Joesler and together they built nearly 500 homes, churches, schools and commercial buildings. They defined what has become known as the "Tucson style," a style which included hand-carved doors, hammered tin and architecture, all reflecting the history and art of both Mexico and southern Arizona. At one time, the Murpheys owned over 8,000 acres in the Catalina Foothills, most of which had been purchased for just a few dollars per acre.

Even real estate tycoons like Murphey can occasionally find themselves in a financial crunch. Following the stock market crash of 1929, Murphey needed to generate cash so that he could pay some of his taxes. He approached the president of the Bisbee Bank in 1930 and offered to sell him land in the foothills of Tucson for five dollars an acre. The banker rejected the offer, saying flat out that no one would ever live on that foothills land except for jack rabbits and coyotes. That same land is worth approximately $100,000 per acre today.

REALTOR

Buying real estate in Tucson was a mess during the 1870s.

Even when a piece of property could be found, it was sometimes impossible to secure a clear title. Real estate was considered so worthless, personal loans were required to complete the purchase.

One of the first real estate firms to specialize in the sale of homes and land in Tucson was Underwood & Gibbons. Deeds and titles were almost incidental throughout the 1860s in Pima County. Offers were made, short-term deeds

2897. A STREET IN OLD TOWN, TUCSON, ARIZ.

Jackson Street in 1910.

The same block in 1998.

executed. More often than not, sales were completed without verifying clear titles. Taxes were seldom paid. Some property owners were at least ten years or more in arrears in payment of taxes.

Underwood & Gibbons tried to sort all this out when they opened their real estate office in Tucson in about 1870. It was a complex, thankless job.

119

RED LIGHT DISTRICT

Tucson's first red light district was a little slice of heaven in a three-block area just north of Congress. The street was called Calle de la India Treiste, or street of the sad Indian girl.

Cribs and sporting houses flourished in the area throughout the 1870s. Passion was usually assessed at about a dollar an hour.

Sabino Street, formerly Gay Alley.

The second district was Maiden Lane. When Congress Street was widened, the earlier area was eliminated and the soiled doves flocked to nests on Gay Alley (Sabino Street).

In 1909, Tucson passed a stiff prostitution ordinance that required the "girls" to have regular medical exams. By the following year, Tucson's tenderloin -- that choice cut of vice -- had sixty-nine prostitutes registered and working the area including Blonde Bella, Minnie Hunter and French Jennie.

Several attempts were made to close the district. One of the most interesting attempts occurred in 1916. A group of citizens approached O.C. Parker, an undertaker, after he had been elected Tucson mayor. When asked if he would close the red light houses, Mayor Parker didn't flinch. He looked the group in the eye and replied they could not count on his support. "Everyone needs a place where they can satisfy their sexual needs," Parker said. He added that Gay Alley was just such a place and he vowed the district would remain open as long as he was mayor. And he kept his promise.

RESTAURANT

During the 1860s, restaurants didn't exist in Tucson. Several of the cantinas served beans with jerked beef in addition to stiff shots of tequila. Tamales were often sold on the streets in season.

The Shoo Fly Restaurant was opened in a one-story adobe building not far from the town's plaza in about 1870. It got its name from the flies there that just wouldn't shoo.

The mud ceiling was covered with muslin to prevent dirt from sifting down onto the tables below. The walls were whitewashed and the floor tamped earth which was sprinkled several times each day to control dust.

Two small Mexican boys stood by the pine tables with large swatters to zap the occasional fly that happened to land within reach.

The menu was fairly limited to frijoles, bacon, an occasional ham and when in season, chiles, onions and fruits from both California and Mexico.

The Shoo Fly Restaurant was the favorite eatery for many of the town's characters. Jack Long was the invention of a local humorist who often swore that when he visited the Shoo Fly, the old codger always ordered a "Jenny Lind steak." If the waiter looked puzzled, Long would explain that a Jenny Lind steak was one "cut from the hoss's upper lip." It was a great story and never failed to get a laugh.

RODEO

Tucson's annual rodeo came about because of a polo player who had a fascination with the traditions of the old west.

Leighton Kramer should have been a cowboy. He loved the western life style and never missed an opportunity to attend a rodeo.

In 1924, while lunching with friends, Kramer said Tucson needed an annual rodeo that offered cash prizes. He had ten acres near Campbell and north of Elm where he sometimes played polo. He offered the site for the event.

The first rodeo there began with street parades downtown, February 21, 1925, and was sponsored by the Arizona Polo Association.

Kramer, wearing a huge cowboy hat, watched the first day's events that included calf roping, steer wrestling and saddle bronc bucking.

By 1927, the rodeo parade budget was $20. Almost all of it was spent that year to hire the Pagago Indian Band. In 1931, La Fiesta de los Vanqueros was sponsored in part by the Tucson Chamber of Commerce and the Pima County Fair Committee.

SALOON

Tucson's first saloons were not much more than dank holes in the wall where a slug of tequila could be purchased for two bits.

Charles O. Brown wanted to own an elegant saloon that was more than just a place to buy a drink. He had a magnificent walnut bar built, installed a brass rail and imported an outstanding selection of whisky and liquors. In 1868, he opened his Congress Hall Saloon on Congress at Meyer Street. It soon became one of the favorite gathering places in town, especially with the members of the Arizona Territorial Legislature.

Charlie Brown and his Congress Hall Saloon.

If Brown's saloon had competition, it was the Palace that flourished just down Meyer Street, south of Broadway. The saloon was located in the Palace Hotel, the first sleeping accommodations in town to feature both a mattress and box springs.

Other popular Tucson saloons included the Bucket of Blood, so named for its garish red interior, the Crystal Palace, the Mesa, the Legal Tender, the Old Stand, the Head Light and the

124

Pueblo. One of the most popular was the Hand & Foster Saloon on Meyer and Mesilla Street. The saloon was co-owned by George Hand who kept dairies that captured the flavor (and boredom) of everyday life in Tucson during the 1870s. Hand's life was filled with whisky, hangovers and frequent visits to the red light district.

SCHOOL BUILDING

The first building actually designed for that purpose was the Congress Street School, located between Scott Street and Sixth Avenue. After a series of raffles, dances and public appeals, the one-story adobe building was completed in about 1876. The main doorway and windows faced Congress Street.

SCHOOL - INDIAN

A school to educate Indian children was established in Tucson by the Presbyterian Church of Home Missions in January of 1888.

Papago Indian School in 1910.

After its first decade of service, the school expanded to include a farm near the Santa Cruz River. Students farmed a 45-acre plot and raised various crops including corn and squash. Surplus vegetables were sold in town to help finance the school. The school enrollment often included more than 100 students at any given time.

SCHOOL - PUBLIC

Tucson High School in 1910.

On November 18, 1867, the Pima County Board of Supervisors created Arizona's first school district. The designated district included "all land within one mile each way from the Plaza de la Masilla," or the town's center at that time.

An old adobe building was found and rented on Pennington Street, not far from Levin's Park. Agustus Brichta was hired as the school's instructor and classes began in January of 1868 with about 55 pupils, all Mexican boys of various ages. All went well for about six months. Then the money ran out. The supervisors refused to provide additional funding so Tucson's first public school closed its doors.

SERVICE STATION

Tucson's first automobile drivers purchased gasoline at George Martin's Drug Store on Congress and Church Street. Gasoline sold by the quart, for about twelve cents per measure.

In 1912, W.E. Felix opened the first drive-through service station at North Sixth at East Tenth. In addition to gasoline and oil, Felix was a mechanic and could repair many of the early automobiles.

SEWING MACHINE

With several small children, Clara Brown saw an immediate need for a sewing machine. Her wish was her husband's command.

Getting a sewing machine to Tucson during the 1860s was no small chore. First, the machine had to be ordered from a firm back east. Then it was shipped by wagon and that might take as long as two or three months in transit. Charles Brown loved his wife and ordered the machine.

The sewing machine arrived from St. Louis and was the envy of Clara's friends.

Brown made a great deal of money during his lifetime. In addition to his popular Congress Hall Saloon at Congress Street and Meyer, he served on Tucson's first city council. The Congress Hall

Saloon was a popular handout for members of the Arizona Territorial Legislature. Some have suggested that the best laws ever passed in Arizona were those which were hatched at Charlie Brown's saloon. When Brown died in 1908, he was virtually penniless. He had made, and spent, several fortunes.

SHOPPING CENTER

Broadway Village.

Developer John Murphey and Architect Josias Joesler built Tucson's first shopping center. Broadway Village at Broadway and Country Club opened in 1939.

Other shopping centers included Swanway, at Swan and Broadway, and Delray on East 22nd Street. Both Swanway and Delray were popular during the 1950s.

SHRINE

Tucson's first shrine was built in the memory of a sinner who died violently and in shame.

Juan Oliveras was a sheep herder during the 1870s. He worked with his father-in-law on a ranch that was just outside of town. Juan's mother-in-law lived in Tucson. One day, Juan was followed to town and discovered in the company of the woman. The father-in-law was so outraged, he grabbed an ax and murdered Juan Oliveras. The young lover was buried in a shallow grave near where he was

128

slain. It would have been a forgotten incident except for one thing. Many people claimed that candles left near the grave, especially those which continued to burn throughout the night, had magical powers. They could make wishes come true.

The present site is not the original. The first Wishing Shrine was near the southwest corner of Meyer Street and West Simpson. The shrine is located today in the 300 block of South Main Street. Candles flicker at the shrine throughout the year but the number seems to increase especially when the Power Ball jackpots do.

The Wishing Shrine.

SKYSCRAPER

Except for city hall and a few churches, most buildings in downtown Tucson were limited to one or two story. In 1929, Tucson got its first skyscraper.

Construction began in 1928. The Pioneer Hotel and Consolidated National Bank Building began climbing toward the sky. When it was topped off in 1929, it was twelve stories. The Consolidated Bank

Building has been a downtown landmark ever since its opening.

It seems logical that the first skyscraper fire would occur in the city's first skyscraper.

Pioneer Hotel.

Consolidated National Bank Building.

During the early morning hours of December 19, 1970, smoke filled the hallways of the Pioneer Hotel. By the time firemen arrived, it was out of control. Twenty-eight people died including Mr.

and Mrs. Albert Steinfeld, of department store fame, who resided in the hotel.

The hotel seemed to be jinxed following the fire. It was finally demolished in 1974. The Consolidated Bank Building was saved.

Tucson's first solar house.

SOLAR HOUSE

Robert W. Bliss Jr. was an associate physicist at the University of Arizona. He designed and built the first solar heated and radiation cooled house in Tucson. It is located at 2023 East Adams Street.

SPEED LIMIT

Although the first automobile didn't arrive in Tucson until about 1901, within two years they had become a problem. Owners of the new gas-buggies raced up and down city streets and were becoming a

131

major hazard, not just to themselves but pedestrians as well.

After several stern warnings from the Police Chief Joe Hopley and Mayor Charles Schumacher, the city council finally took action. The city's first speed limit was quickly passed in 1903 prohibiting drivers from excelling faster than seven miles per hour on city streets.

Some driver's paid little attention to the new law and that's when the city's first speeding tickets were issued. Police officers cracked down on fast and reckless drivers, especially those that used Speedway Blvd. as a racetrack to test the speed of their machines.

In 1913, the city relented a little and raised the speed limit to ten miles per hour.

In 1918, there were 1,800 automobiles registered throughout the state of Arizona.

STOCK BROKER

William A. Scott Jr. opened a small brokerage office at 13 Meyer Street during the spring of 1882. In addition to bonds, he offered selected stocks issued by California, Nevada and Arizona companies.

STORE - ANGLO

Solomon Warner, who as an adult had a striking resemblance to President U.S. Grant, was born in 1811 in New York. In 1855, he found work constructing foundation walls at Fort Yuma and managed to save enough of his wages to purchase a small inventory of retail goods.

He loaded his inventory into wagons, arriving in Tucson in March 2, 1856, just eleven days after Mexican troops had vacated the Presidio. He found a small adobe hut just outside the west gate of the Presidio and there, he opened "The American Store." It was the first retail store owned by an American citizen, stocked with goods that had originated in the United States. His store opened March 10, 1856.

SWIMMING POOL

Although it was common practice to swim in irrigation ditches, Helen Wetmore was a determined little girl and she wanted a swimming pool. In 1918, he coaxed her uncle into enlarging a ditch at the family home now the site of the present day Tucson Mall. A concrete bottom and sides were constructed which expanded the swimming area to 15x30 feet. It was fed by a nearby well, requiring the water to be flushed several times each week.

Mission Pool opened later that same year. It was located on the southeast corner of Mission Road and Ajo Way. The Mission Pool was also made of concrete and had a water depth of about eight feet on the deepest end. The pool was demolished during the 1940s.

TELEGRAPH

Telegraph wires in 1874 connected

The Western Union Office on Congress during the 1930s.

Tucson with the outside world as never before. After the completion of wires between Tucson and San Diego, news and communications were instant.

Western Union opened at 18 East Congress. The Postal Telegraph Office, a competitor, opened next door at 16 East Congress.

The local Western Union Office closed in 1984.

134

TELEPHONE

The Tucson Weekly Star connected a telephone line between its editorial offices and the Western Union Office in March of 1881. It was the first commercial use of the telephone in southern Arizona.

Charles Lord was postmaster and when he became president of the Arizona Telephone Company, he had a small "central exchange" built in the rear of the post office building on Congress Street. An operator was hired to monitor some 20 subscribers and telephone service began April 1, 1881.

By 1888, the Tucson Telephone Company had expanded to the point that new, larger quarters were necessary. The company moved to the old fire bell tower on Church Plaza. Within six years, 150 Tucson homes and businesses were connected to the system. A long distance call was possible after 1903 when telephone lines connected Tucson with Nogales.

The Tucson system was purchased by the Mountain States Telephone and Telegraph Company in 1912. At the time of the acquisition, there were 1,200 telephones in Tucson.

TELEVISION

On the 13th hour of the 13th day of January, 1953, switches were flipped and KOPO-TV, Channel 13, signed on the air for its first day of broadcasting. Paul Plunkett, a vice-president of the company, introduced the staff of KOPO, during its first hour on the air. Plunkett also doubled during those first few months as the station's weatherman. The studios were at 115 West Drachman.

Although KOPO-TV had won the race to be the first Tucson television station on the air, it had been a photo finish. KVOA-TV was Tucson's second station and was on the air by September of the same year.

Tucson's love affair with television was instant and passionate. Program favorites included Beat the Clock, Sky King, Schlitz Playhouse of Stars, the Big Picture, Industry on Parade and, yes, wrestling. Remember the antics of Gorgeous George?

TELEVISION - EDUCATIONAL

An application was submitted to the FCC on May 2, 1958, asking permission to construct an education television station at the University of Arizona. The 250-foot tower was completed that November. The station was expected to have a 20-mile coverage area with a power of about 1,000 watts.

KUAT-TV, Channel 6, began broadcasting March 8, 1959, from a small studio in Herring Hall on the University campus. The first program guide was published in October of 1961.

TELEVISION PERSONALITY

The earliest television personality to connect with viewers was Virginia Mittendorf. Her "Visiting with Virginia" was a blend of news, guest interviews and even an occasional recipe. Her program was aired Monday through Friday on KOPO-TV, Channel 13, beginning in February of 1953.

Virginia and her co-host, Jerry O'Brien, chatted between musical interludes provided by Dude Vance on the Hammond Organ. The set included comfortable living room furniture that helped set the mood. "Visiting with Virginia" was live and featured an audience. Her final broadcast was in 1964 when she retired.

THANKSGIVING CELEBRATION

Charley Brown was a prosperous saloon owner. When he and his wife, Clara, moved into a new home in November of 1868, they decided to celebrate by having both a traditional house warming and a Thanksgiving feast.

The morning began when a priest blessed the new home, which even after 130 years still stands in downtown Tucson at 40 West Broadway. After the blessing, the feast. Venison, which had been slowly smouldering in a pit near the patio, was carried to the table. Other Thanksgiving delicacies that day included Indian corn, squash, tortillas, oysters from the Gulf of California and a creamy custard, sweetened with honey from Hermosillo. After the feast, Charley and his 20 or so guests adjourned with eggnog and French brandy in hand to the patio. Someone had brought a violin so the evening was spent dancing to reels and even an occasional polka.

As the evening became night, the Browns and their friends gathered around the dying embers of the fire for a final toast. So ended Tucson's earliest Thanksgiving of record.

Charley Brown was an interesting man. In 1868, he opened the Congress Hall Saloon, then located on Congress at Meyer Street. It was a popular watering hole, especially for the thirsty members of the Territorial Legislature, then based in Tucson. The legislators and the saloon were a perfect match. In fact, some even now claim that the best laws ever passed in Arizona were those which were hatched in the smokey legislative roost of Charley's Congress Hall Saloon.

Charley was fascinated by new gadgets and modern conveniences. When his wife became pregnant in 1870, he ordered a baby carriage from a company in St. Louis. His growing family created a need for a bathtub and he soon had one installed which was made of zinc. Although the tub had to be hand-filled, it was nothing short of a marvel, especially at a time when most people in Tucson bathed -- when the mood struck them -- in the nearest irrigation ditch. Clara loved music and a piano was next on the Brown family agenda. A piano soon arrived and it wasn't just any piano but a Steinway square grand that had been carefully shipped from the east by wagon. By 1875, Clara had become the envy of her friends when she got a sewing machine. All of these marvelous things were firsts -- not just in Tucson -- but throughout the Territory of Arizona as well.

Clara and Charley Brown raised four sons and a daughter in the house. As the family expanded, so did the house. The earliest portion of the Charley Brown house is the wing that is nearest to Jackson Street. It was built during the 1860s, possibly even a decade earlier. This area had a parlor, dining

138

room, four bedrooms and a small kitchen. An addition, which fronted Camp Street, now Broadway, was completed in 1876. The improvements included an impressive front entryway, a formal parlor and several bedrooms in addition to a bathroom for Charley's bathtub. The rooms featured gaslights, at least two Victorian fireplace mantels and that real rarity in Arizona -- wallpaper. The floors were mostly packed earth.

Brown died in 1908 and after several close calls, the family home was saved. The Charley Brown house is currently owned and maintained by the Arizona Historical Society. The structure is listed on the National Register of Historic Places.

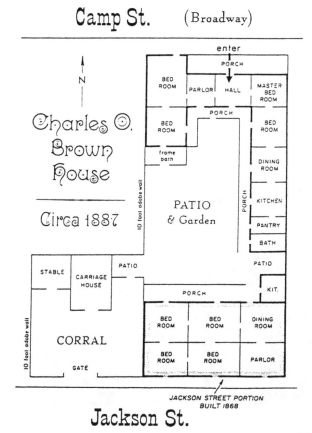

Camp St. (Broadway)

Charles O. Brown House

Circa 1887

N

enter

PORCH

BED ROOM | PARLOR | HALL | MASTER BED ROOM

PORCH

BED ROOM | | BED ROOM

frame bath | | DINING ROOM

10 foot adobe wall

PATIO & Garden

PORCH

KITCHEN

PANTRY

BATH

STABLE | CARRIAGE HOUSE | PATIO | | PATIO

PORCH | KIT.

10 foot adobe wall

CORRAL

GATE

BED ROOM | BED ROOM | DINING ROOM

BED ROOM | BED ROOM | PARLOR

JACKSON STREET PORTION BUILT 1868

Jackson St.

139

THEATRE

Alexander Levin built a small hall in his park near the foot of Pennington Street during the 1870s. It was the first building constructed as a theatre in the territory. The opening night production at Levin's Hall was "Grand Concert," a heart-wrenching melodrama featuring local players.

The theatre was popular. It also was unstable. After less than five months, the earthen roof collapsed but Levin's Hall was quickly rebuilt on the same site. The first production in the new theatre was "H.M.S. Pinafore," a crowd pleaser starring members of Pring's Opera Company.

In 1882, the theatre again closed for extensive remodeling. That October, Jay Rial's Theatre Company presented "Uncle Tom's Cabin." Patrons noticed boxes, a gallery and an enlarged stage in the newly named Park Theatre. The last performance occurred there during the summer of 1884.

During the 1890s, the theatre was used first as an armory and later a meeting hall. It was finally demolished in 1909.

THEATRE - SPANISH

Teatro Carmen was Tucson's first theatre devoted exclusively to Spanish drama. It was named for its founder, Carmen Soto Vasquez. The theatre opened with great fanfare the evening of May 20, 1915.

The theatre was at 384 South Meyer Street. Dramatic productions continued in the building until 1922. Later, the theatre hosted movies, concerts and even an occasional boxing match. It was eventually used as an Elk's Lodge.

Teatro Carmen in 1998.

TOURISTS

As Mexican soldiers celebrated the New Year's Eve of 1826 at the Presidio in Tucson, three American trappers suddenly appeared at the gate. Manuel de Leon, the commander of the Presidio, welcomed the exhausted visitors. After checking their papers, the three men rested and then were on their way.

Were they lost or did they visit the Presidio by design. Because of the sketchy records of the time, the details will never be known for certain. The trappers were in the area, no doubt lured by the rich pelts of the Sonoran beaver. Whether by design or by accident, the three trappers came to the attention of Juan Romero, Tucson's third constitutional mayor. He sent a report to his superiors in Mexico that mentioned the New Year's Eve visit. Despite the lack of historic details, the three men were the first American citizens to visit the Presidio.

Sunny winter vacations
in the old haunts of the Conquistadors
TUCSON
("Too-sŏh'n")

TOURS BY AIR

Walter Douglas was the grandson and son of men who found their fortunes underground. Walter found his future in the skies.

Douglas was raised in a family of executives who were involved in mineral exploration for the Phelps Dodge Corporation. During then 1920s, Walter learned to fly an airplane and enjoyed it so much, he used inherited money to establish Gilpin Airlines in San Francisco. He moved his charter service to Tucson following the stock market crash of 1929.

Douglas purchased 400 acres of flat desert land on Roger Road in northwest Tucson. By 1936, he had built a small airport and was offering both charter tours and flight instruction. During WWII, Gilpin Air Field became an important training facility for pilots in the U.S. Army Air Corps.

Urban sprawl brought an end to the airfield. In 1959 he sold his property to developers. He died in 1987 at the age of 76.

Gilpin Field in 1938.

TRAFFIC LIGHT

With more and more automobiles jamming the downtown streets, it didn't take city officials long to realize some sort of control had to be found. The traffic light was the solution.

The city's first traffic light was installed March 14, 1927, at the congested intersection of Congress and Sixth Avenue, long considered one of the most dangerous in town.

Before traffic lights became commonplace, drivers would approach intersections, hit the gas and then try to race the other drivers through, a technique that is used in Tucson even today.

UNDERTAKER

Sam Baird opened his first undertaking parlor on West Congress Street in 1870. His  establishment had all the necessary trappings including a hearse.

144

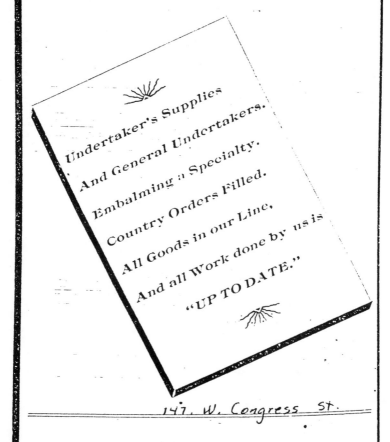
Sam Baird's Undertaking Parlor, circa 1890.

A "front parlor" funeral in 1910.

Baird's Funeral Parlor was purchased in 1898 by Olva Clayton Parker. Parker was from Tennessee and worked in Phoenix several years before relocating to Tucson. Parker became politically involved and was elected Tucson's mayor in 1917. He served until 1922 and was responsible for establishing the city's municipal airport.

Parker was considered an innovator in mortuary circles. He was the first state director to be licensed by Arizona and a progressive businessman. He introduced the first motorized hearse here in 1909 and was the first director to offer a full-range of mortuary services. He lived at 540 North Main Street.

UNIVERSITY

It was 1885 and the time had come for the Arizona Territorial Legislature meeting in Prescott to pass out the goodies.

146

C.C. Stephens was a delegate from Tucson. Just before he left for the session, he was given a wad of

One of the earliest pictures of Old Main. circa 1895.

University cadets take a brief time out near the horticulturist's college in about 1900.

money and told to get the capitol for Tucson -- or else.

Stephens was powerless. By the time he arrived in Prescott, the deals had already been cut. He glumly watched as the capitol was awarded to Prescott. The prison, which was considered a real moneymaker, was presented to Yuma. Phoenix got another plum, the state insane asylum. The treat bag was almost empty. The only thing left was the university and it was given to Tucson almost as an afterthought. Stephens knew it was going to be an almost impossible job to convince the good citizens of Tucson that having a university wasn't such a bad idea after all but even he was shocked by the response he got when he returned to the Old Pueblo.

As he stood on the stage of the Opera House, he tried to duck the rotten fruit and vegetables being thrown at him. As the crowd jeered, one of the town's bartenders shouted "Who in the hell wants a university, professors don't even drink." When someone threw a dead cat onto the stage, it was the last straw. Stephens had seen and heard enough. He left the Opera House but was so shaken, he hired a body guard. He then waited until some of the more vocal opponents in town had had a chance to cool.

Many of those most opposed to the school had second thoughts when the legislature dangled a check for $25,000 in front of the good people of Tucson several months later. Like all government money there was a little catch. The $25,000 had to be used to secure land for the new university and it had to be accomplished within a year. If Tucson failed to find and secure the land, the money would be forfeited so the search was on.

A patch of desolate, desert land was found about three miles east of the center of town. One of the men on the land committee was, ironically, a saloon keeper. It was secured and construction started in October of 1887.

VIEW OF TUCSON

J. Ross Browne completed a sketch of Tucson in 1864 for his book "Adventures in the Apache Country." The book was published in 1869 and is one the first views of the layout of Tucson, if not the first.

WAITER

The Shoo Fly Restaurant was probably the first in Tucson to hire an employee responsible for food orders, serving and clearing tables. The Palace Hotel went one step further. The Palace dressed its waiters in uniforms and even trained them in the fine arts of such things as wine selection. W.H. Lewis and W.W. Douglas were both waiters at the Palace Hotel during the early 1880s. Both knew their wines and could even dazzle customers by mumbling a few words of French. George Hanoviller and Henry L. Martin were also waiters during the 1880s and worked at Porter's Hotel.

WATER

Even more precious than gold in the old west, was water.

The Little Eye Spring is virtually impossible to locate today but during the earliest years of settlement in Tucson, it provided one of the best sources of drinking water in the area. Father Kino certainly must have paused to refresh himself at the spring when he visited here over 200 years ago.

The spring was located just west of the present day Wishing Shrine near Main Avenue and Simpson

Street. When the Presidio was completed in 1776, Little Eye was abandoned since it was outside the protective walls and was considered unsafe.

By 1855, attitudes had changed and shifted again. Burros were driven down Main Street to the springs where containers were filled with water. The water was then sometimes sold for about five cents a gallon by vendors. When a household purchased water, a pencil mark was scratched on the front door jam. At the end of each month, the scratches were added up and the water bill was then due and payable. Most people were honest and it was a simple system that worked.

Near Little Eye Springs.

By the 1860s, most water used for washing and cleaning came from wells scattered throughout the area. Drinking water was drawn from natural springs near Elysian Grove and again sold for about five cents a gallon.

The first flow of water through municipal mains was a day of great celebration. A large crowd gathered near a tap at Congress and Main the morning of September 6, 1882. Just before noon, the crowd cheered as water began to trickle -- then gush -- through the tap.

WATER SYSTEM

The father of the modern Tucson water system was an engineer from Albuquerque.

Sylvester Watts was hired in 1881 by Tucson to plan a municipal water system. By the following year, the first mains were not just planned but functioning. A crude sewer system followed.

Even though some lucky Tucson homeowners had municipal water as early as 1883, the first bathtub with running water was not installed in a private home until almost 20 years later.

WHIPPING POST

The Spaniards had a simple tool in dealing with soldiers and civilians who misbehaved -- a whipping post. The first one was installed near the southwest corner of the Presidio just a few steps from the jail. Traces of the old jail were found during the construction of the Pima County Courthouse in 1928.

After the Gadsden Purchase in 1855 and the withdrawal of Mexican soldiers at the Presidio, Tucson quickly gained a reputation for being lawless.

Crime was so out of control, Mark Aldrich and a group of other concerned citizens met during the summer of 1860 to try and establish a set of workable laws for the town. Aldrich was appointed judge and a whipping post was once again erected near the town plaza for those who violated the rules. The system was a simple one. If a man was sentenced to 20 lashes at the whipping post, he was usually given ten licks and then told to return the next day for the rest. The culprit usually cleared out of town that very night instead of waiting around for more lashes. That was the idea but even the whipping post failed to improve the streets of Tucson much.

A writer for Harper's Magazine, reported in 1863 that Tucson "was a place of resort for traders, speculators, thieves, murderers and vagrant politicians." Sort of like today.

Aldrich was disgusted and he quit. The whipping post was discontinued sometime after the town incorporated in 1873.

YOUNG MEN'S CHRISTIAN ASSOCIATION

The first YMCA in Tucson opened in 1914 at 125 West Congress Street. The main floor of the building had a spacious lobby, a gym and a card room. The lower level had both a bowling alley and a swimming pool.

The YMCA building was demolished in 1966. The Pima County Health Department now occupies the site.

ZOO

It wasn't exactly a zoo. It was more like a private collection.

When Leopoldo Carrillo opened Elysian Grove on South Main Avenue, he maintained a small collection of animals for the amusement of his visitors. The animals included a rather grumpy bear, a wildcat and an assortment of birds. The small menagerie was being displayed as early as 1875.

*From fine shade trees to croquet, Levin's
Park had it all.*

AUTOMOBILE DEALERS (1920)

Babbit Brothers
North Stone Avenue at Alameda

Pedro Camacho Automobile Company
399 South Meyer

D.M. Caudill
215 East Congress

Monte Mansfield Ford
19 East Broadway

O.R. Maynard
70 North Sixth

Ryland & Olcott Studebaker
355 Toole Avenue

Snow & Tufts Oldsmobile
and Chevrolet
221 East Broadway

Southern Arizona Buick
125 North Sixth Avenue

Williamson-Bailey
Hudson, Maxwell & Essex Automobiles
125 South Scott

White Motor Company
Scott at Broadway

CENSUS

Year	Tucson	Arizona
1821	395	
1831	465	
1860	929	
1864	1,568	4,573
1870	3,224	9,568
1880	7,007	40,440
1890	5,150	88.243
1900	7,531	122,931
1910	13,193	204,354
1920	20,292	334,162
1930	32,506	435,573
1940	36,818	499,261
1950	45,454	749,587
1960	212,892	1,302,161
1970	262,933	1,770,900
1980	350,537	2,719,000
1990	402,506	3,665,228

CITY OF TUCSON FIRE CHIEFS

Jack Boylen	1881-1886 & 1890-1898
Joe Encinas	1886-1890
Frank Russell	1898-1903
G.K. Smith	1903-1904
Henry Melluish	1904-1905
George Scholfield	1905-1909
Sam Barkley	1909-1910
Tom Conlin	1910-1911
Frank Ganz	1911-1915
Harry Parker	1915-1921
Joseph Roberts	1921-1937
Henry L. Hilles	1937-1946
J.C. Sievert	1946-1953
John H. Freeman	1953-1966
L.F. Peterson	1966-1976
E. Dean Holland	1976-1982
Richard M. Moreno	1982-1993
Fred L. Shipman	1993-Present

TUCSON MARSHALS

Jimmy Douglas (1869)
Served as Officer of the Court for Justice of the Peace Charles Meyer.

William Morgan (May 17, 1871 - June 14, 1871)

John Miller (July 24, 1871 - January 5, 1873)

Francis Hodges (January 6, 1873 - March 8, 1873)

John Thayer (March 13, 1873 - May 8, 1873)

Francisco Esparza (May 8, 1873 - January 4, 1875)

David Davis (January 5, 1875 - February 12, 1875)

Francisco Esparza (February 23, 1875 - January 3, 1876)

TUCSON CHIEFS OF POLICE

A.G. Buttner (January 4, 1876 - February 7, 1877)
Isaac Brokaw (February 27, 1877 - July 16, 1877)
A.G. Buttner (July 16, 1877 - January 6, 1879)
Isaac Brokaw (January 7, 1879 - January 3, 1881)
A.G. Buttner (January 4, 1881 - May 6, 1883)
Nathan Appel (May 7, 1883 - August 6, 1883)+
A.G. Buttner (August 6, 1883 - January 8, 1884)
Mathew Johnson (January 9, 1884 - January 5, 1885)
A.G. Buttner (January 6, 1885 - November 6, 1885)
William Roche (November 7, 1885 - May 18, 1893)
Lucas Estrella (June 5, 1893 - August 7, 1893)
John Zimmerman (January 1, 1894 - March 5, 1894)
Robert Paul (April 5, 1894 - December 31, 1896)
Sam Finley (January 1, 1897 - June 6, 1898)
George Oakes (June 7, 1898 - December 31, 1898)
William Taylor (January 1, 1899 - December 31, 1902)
Joseph Hopley (January 1, 1903 - January 4, 1909)
Nabor Pacheco (January 4, 1909 - December 31, 1909)
Patrick Flanagan (January 1, 1910 - May 12, 1910)
Frank E. Murphy (May 28, 1910 - December 31, 1910)
Judson Arnold (January 1, 1911 - December 31, 1912)
John Rolfing (January 1, 1913 - December 31, 1914)
James Cullen (January 1, 1915 - December 31, 1916)
E.D. Mills (January 1, 1917 - February 15, 1917)
Frank Bailey (March 5, 1917 - April 15, 1920)
Joseph Hopley (August 9, 1920 - December 31, 1920)
Dallas Ford (January 1, 1921 - December 31, 1924)

TUCSON POLICE CHIEFS (continued)

John Dyer (January 1, 1925 - September 6, 1933)++
Christopher Wollard (October 6, 1933 - October 22, 1938)
Henry Hilles (October 22, 1938 - July 3, 1939)
Don Hays (July 3, 1939 - August 13, 1940)
Harold Wheeler (November 18, 1940 - December 11, 1944)
Jesse Ingle (January 1, 1945 - September 18, 1945)
Don Hays (September 22, 1945 - January 25, 1957)
Paul H. Bohardt (October 10, 1956 - June 14, 1957)+
Bernard Garmire (June 15, 1957 - June 1, 1969)
William Gilkinson (June 1, 1969 - June 15, 1969)+
William Gilkinson (September 30, 1969 - October 26, 1981
Peter Ronstadt (October 27, 1981 - February 24, 1992)
Elaine Hedke (March 2, 1992 - November 15, 1993)+++
Michael Ulichney (November 15, 1993 - June 6, 1994) +
Douglas Smith (June 6, 1994 - October 6, 1998)
Richard Miranda (October 6, 1998 - Present)

+ Acting
++ John Dyer was the last Police Chief to be elected.   After Dyer, all chiefs were selected through civil service appointments.
+++ Tucson's first female Chief of Police

MAYORS OF TUCSON

Sidney Randolph DeLong	1871-1873
James H. Toole	1873-1875
Estevan Ochoa	1875-1876
John Brackett Allen	1876-1878
James H. Toole	1878-1880
Robert N. Leatherwood	1880-1881
John Sterling Carr	1881-1882
Pinckney Randolph Tully	1882-1883
Charles Moses Straus	1883-1884
Andrew Cronley	1884-1885
George Rayfield	1885-1887
W.E. Stevens	1887-1889
Frederick Maish	1889-1893
W.I. Perry	1893-1895
Henry H. Buehman	1895-1899
Gust A. Hoff	1899-1901
Charles F. Schumacher	1901-1905
Levi H. Manning	1905-1907
Charles F. Slack	1907-1909
George Benjamin Heney	1909 (Jan 3-Nov 4)
Preston N. Jacobus	1909-1911
Ira Erven Huffman	1911-1915
J. Knox Corbett	1915-1916
Olva Clayton Parker	1917-1921
Rudolph Rasmessen	1921-1925
John E. White	1925-1928
Frank J. Cordis	1928 (nine months)
W.A. Julian	1929-1931
George Kendell Smith	1931-1933
Henry O. Jaastad	1933-1947
Elbert Thompson Houston	1947-1950
J.O. Niemann	1950-1951
Fred Emery	1951-1955
Don Hummel	1955-1961
Lewis W. Davis	1961-1967
James N. Corbett Jr.	1967-1971

TUCSON MAYORS (cont.)

Lewis C. Murphy	1971-1987
Tom Volgy	1987-1991
George Miller	1991-Present

There's Sunshine
all Winter in
TUCSON

TELEVISION STATIONS (1957)

KDWI-TV
2173 North Sixth Avenue

KOPO-TV
115 West Drachman

KVOA-TV
209 West Elm

TUCSON HARNESS AND SADDLE HOUSE.

A large and Well Selected Stock of

Harness, Saddles, Bridles, Horse and Carriage Furnishings Always on Hand.

We Manufacture on Order

Anything Desired on our Line . . .

The Prices are Right for the
Class of Goods Sold.

. KINDLY GIVE US A CALL .

V. M. CORDOVA,

196 WEST CONGRESS ST.

Proprietor.

TUCSON THEATRES

1920
Carmen Theatre (380 South Meyer)
Lyric (135 West Congress)
Pima Theatre (34 West Congress)
Royal Theatre (320 South Meyer)
The Tucson Opera House (49 East Congress)

1930
Fox (17 West Congress)
Fox Lyric (161 West Congress)
The Opera House (49 East Congress)
Rialto (318 East Congress)
Royal (320 South Meyer)
Temple (330 South Scott)

1940
Fox (21 West Congress)
Fox Lyric (161 West Congress)
Plaza (132 West Congress)
Rialto (318 East Congress)
Rio (320 South Meyer)
State (51 East Congress)
Temple (300 South Scott)
The Tucson Little Theatre (20 West Ochoa)

1950
Biltmore Motor Vu (600 West Indio)
Catalina (2320 North Campbell)
Fox-Lyric (161 West Congress)
Fox-Tucson (17 West Congress)
Midway Drive-In (4500 East Speedway)
Paramount (318 East Congress)
Plaza (132 West Congress)
State Theatre (51 East Congress)

UNIVERSITY OF ARIZONA PRESIDENTS

The office of President for the University of Arizona was created by the Board of Regents May 30, 1894.   F.A. Gulley served until the first President was named during the spring of 1894.

T.B. Comstock	1894-1895
H. Billman	1895-1897
M.M. Parker	1897-1901
F.Y. Adams	1902-1903
F.C. Babcock	1903-1910
A.H. Wilde	1911-1914
R.B. von Kleinsmid	1914-1921
C.H. Marvin	1922-1927
B. Cummings	1927-1928
H.L. Shantz	1928-1936
P.S. Burgess	1936-1937
A. Atkinson	1937-1947
J.B. McCormick	1947-1951
R.A. Harvill	1951-1971
J.P Schaefer	1971-1982
H. Koffler	1982-1991
M.T. Pacheco	1991-1997
Peter Likins	1997-Present

EARLY TUCSON NEWSPAPERS

The Arizonian (1859)
The Citizen (1877)
The Tucson Bulletin-Star (1877)
Las Dos Republicas (1877)
El Fronterizo (1878)
La Sonora (1879)
El Alcaran (1879)
The Record (1879)
The Arizona Daily Star (1879)
Arizona Quarterly (1880)
Illustrated Enterprise (1881)
The Journal (1881)
The Mining Index (1883)
The Arizona Livestock Journal (1884)
Sunshine and Silver (1884)
Beef and Bullion (1885)
The Tailings (1885)
The Times (1885)

HE WEEKLY ARIZONIAN.

ARD WELLS, Editor and Proprietor.   TUCSON, ARIZONA, AUGUST 4, 1859.   VOL. 1.—No. 2